The Radical Christian

'The axe is laid to the root of the tree'

ARTHUR WALLIS

KINGSWAY PUBLICATIONS
EASTBOURNE

ISBN 0 86065 162 2

Unless otherwise stated, biblical quotations are from
the New International Version,
© New York International Bible Society 1978.
AV = Authorized (King James) Version (crown copyright)
JB = Jerusalem Bible
© Darton Longman & Todd Ltd 1966, 1967, 1968
RSV = Revised Standard Version
copyright 1946, 1952, © 1971, 1973 by the
Division of Christian Education of the National
Council of the Churches of Christ in the USA

Printed in Great Britain for
KINGSWAY PUBLICATIONS LTD
Lottbridge Drove, Eastbourne, E. Sussex BN23 6NT by
Richard Clay (The Chaucer Press) Ltd, Bungay, Suffolk.
Typesetting by Nuprint Services Ltd, Harpenden, Herts.

TO
my brothers and colleagues in the work
of the kingdom who have exemplified in
their ministry so many of the principles
set forth in this book,
    with affection and gratitude.

CONTENTS

THANK-YOUS

To Tony Pearce for kindly allowing me to use his testimony in Chapter 3.

To Edgar Parkyns for shafts of light through a tape of his on the history of the early church.

To Alan Boardman for the map on page 173.

To Peggy Burns for her speedy and efficient typing of the manuscript.

To David Matthew, Stanley Jebb and Bryn Jones for going through the manuscript and offering valuable suggestions.

To my brothers and sisters in the Otley housegroup, who helped me by their prayers and encouraged me with their enquiries.

To my fellow elders of the church in Bradford who eased the load during the final months of writing.

Lastly, but most importantly, to my wife, Eileen, my most faithful critic and best encourager, who painstakingly checked every chapter and every reference, and also helped me with research.

Introduction:
PUTTING AN AXE
TO THE ROOT

A large number of Christians who have been at some time involved in the movement of the Holy Spirit are now finding themselves in a 'post-charismatic vacuum', and may even be suffering from 'post-charismatic depression'. This is no reflection on the genuineness of their experience or the personal blessing that came from it. It is just that some of them did not realize that their experience of the Holy Spirit was never intended by God to be more than a stage post in their spiritual pilgrimage. Others fully understood this, but their 'vacuum' exists because they have never got a clear answer to the question—'A stage post to where?'

In the early days people talked about 'the charismatic movement'. Then it became 'the charismatic renewal', or 'the renewal movement'. Now people seem to be content to call it 'the renewal'. Along the way we seem to have lost 'charismatic' and 'movement', the two words that we had at the start. Just coincidence? A mere change of terminology? Or something more significant?

Ebbing Tide

Apart from the charismatic Catholics, 'the renewal' in

denominational churches peaked in the late seventies, and is now unmistakably in decline. Though many reasons may be put forward, there is one that I believe to be paramount. It is a deficiency that is common to Christians in general. It was one cause of many non-charismatics shrinking from a personal encounter with the Holy Spirit in the first instance. And it has now overtaken and largely halted the charismatic movement. I refer to the *absence of biblical radicalism*.

The Israelites who came out of Egypt were all charismatic. Daily they witnessed and experienced the supernatural power of God. But lack of this radical quality caused them to come to a halt before they had attained their inheritance—all except that pair of radicals, Caleb and Joshua, who followed the Lord wholeheartedly.

Calling a Spade a Spade

To talk about 'the absence of biblical radicalism' probably leaves most of us untouched because we don't quite know what it means. Let's call this malaise by its true name—*compromise*. This has been defined as 'the partial surrender of one's position, for the sake of coming to terms' (Oxford Dictionary). For the Christian it means that he concedes something that God has given, or sets aside something that God has revealed, for the sake of coming to terms with the situation that he faces. It may mean bowing to some convention, clinging to some prejudice or defending some tradition. It may be an attempt to accommodate someone else's wishes or to curry someone's favour. Or it may be to preserve reputation or earn 'respectability'. When we are dealing with truth, if there is concession there is compromise.

Some who are careful not to compromise when God shows them his way for their personal lives, fail when God shows them his way for their church life. Others do not even realize that God has definite things to say about this. Hopefully this book will help to remedy that. But once we clearly see God's will and God's way in this area, our failure to give a radical response is as much compromise as if it concerned our personal walk with God.

We never compromise out of ignorance, only out of knowledge. The temptation does not arise until God reveals truth to our hearts. It was obedience to new truth that brought the charismatic movement into being. It was failure to give continuing obedience to further revelation that has brought it to a halt. Men who had taken radical and costly steps of obedience at the beginning began to shilly-shally. They were not sure that they wanted to go where God might be leading. They applied the brakes— and the movement ground to a halt. But God moved on.

The Radical Remedy

When Jesus told his disciples that he was heading for the cross Peter told him, 'Spare yourself.' Compromise is that inner whisper of the self-life that would turn us from the path of total, unswerving obedience to the will of God. Jesus was not deflected, because the cross was not only his destination but a principle working within him. The cross is still the radical and sharp instrument God uses to deal, not only with compromise, but with every other manifestation of the self-life.

The flesh is against the Spirit and the Spirit against the flesh. Where there is no emphasis on the work of the cross in the life of the believer—and there has been all too little in the charismatic movement—the flesh is left undisturbed to oppose the work of the Spirit. Here is a major reason for the waning of the Spirit's power.

True radicalism is a product of the cross. It is only as we willingly embrace the cross that the axe is laid to the root of all within us that is opposed to the deep working of the

Holy Spirit. The cross is therefore the underlying theme of this book.

A word to those who believe that they have not compromised what God has shown them, and that they are continuing in the current move of God. Even if that is true, remember that you have not yet come to your rest and your inheritance. The journey is not yet over. You can win today and lose tomorrow. 'So, if you think you are standing firm, be careful that you don't fall.' 'So do not become proud, but stand in awe.' There is more to be revealed. New challenges to radical obedience lie further down the road. It's not enough to be marching on in the move of God. Make sure that the cross is still at work within you.

Demanding a Verdict

If it is true that God has moved on, where is he now? If he has a fresh word, something that he was not saying when the charismatic movement began in the mid-sixties, what is that word? If God is still moving, where is he headed? If we have got left behind, how can we catch up? These are some of the questions that this book seeks to answer.

It has not been an easy word to bring. It will not be an easy word to receive. It will not leave the reader in a comfortable place of neutrality. It will call for a verdict. It is needful to remember that whenever we give a verdict on God's truth we give a verdict on ourselves. The response of the reader to whatever God may say to him in this book will determine whether he is a compromiser or a radical.

The axe is laid to the root of the tree.

1

MEET THE RADICAL

Through the smoke that drifted across the Students Union you could see him, talking animatedly to a group of his cronies. Hair falling somewhat untidily to his shoulders, a loud check shirt unbuttoned, well-patched jeans, and a pair of leather sandals that had seen better days, all combined to tell you that this young man had no concern about his appearance, except to make sure that no one would think he looked 'respectable'.

For the leisure activities that filled the time of most of his fellow students he couldn't care less. But you would find him ready at the drop of a hat to discuss with you, or anyone else who would listen, his one passionate concern— the basic injustices and inequalities of our modern society, and how it *must* be—it *will* be overthrown, by violence if necessary. His tone changes from anger to animation as he goes on to speak of the new order that is to come, a world in which these gross injustices would at last be righted.

We have more than a sneaking suspicion that if our young radical were one day to be let loose on society, he would be much more successful in tearing down than building up. In any case, the demolition of the old is always so much easier than the construction of anything new and better. But the sober fact that his youthful optimism prevents him seeing, is that the termites that he has spotted in the old structures have already invaded the timbers with which he would build the new.

His reactions to the hypocrisy, injustice and self-interest of the old order may be justified, but he cannot see that whatever he tries to build, the arrogance and anger, the intolerance and violence that are already motivating him, will inevitably bring forth fruit after their own kind, and in the end destroy his 'brave new world'.

Can You Identify?

In a word, the radicalism of this radical is not radical enough. It only addresses itself to the externals of the human problem, such as social structures, standards of living, distribution of wealth and such like, and leaves the root untouched. The new order would only prove to be 'the bad old days', having discarded open-neck shirt and slacks, now dressed in a new uniform of drab grey.

We may be tempted to feel that we have nothing in common with 'the angry young man' who is for ever rebelling against authority, protesting against the status quo, or undermining 'the establishment'. He is a fanatic totally dedicated to his ideals, and therefore not amenable to reason. After all, it is surely our duty to submit to the governing authorities and to lead 'a peacable and quiet life'. Are not rulers ordained by God? And is not this the reason why we are to submit to their authority? Yet, though the spirit of the militant radical may be totally alien to the Spirit of Christ, there is a principle that he demonstrates in his worldly way that has its spiritual counterpart in the kingdom of God.

Birth of a Word

Over the years 'radicalism' has developed its own specific

meanings, but it was not until about 1780 that it invaded the arena of British politics, being used to describe someone who advocated 'radical parliamentary reform', which was nothing more sinister than the right of all men to vote. In due course radicalism was used to describe any kind of political extremism.

Radical Theologians

This political use of the word is also applied to theologians who have accepted certain political and social ideologies which they proclaim as the 'now' word, the prophetic message for the church. Michael Harper in the Ashe Lecture for 1979 said, 'Much radical theology is based on a false view of the kingdom, identifying it far too simplistically with the here-and-now, and not profoundly enough with either the future or with the present reality of the church.'

There should certainly be genuine and practical concern on the part of committed Christians for the betterment of mankind, and for the rectifying of political and social injustice, and all too often they have completely neglected this area, feeling that it was no concern of theirs. Of recent years there has been a big re-think going on, especially on the part of evangelicals, though this does not mean that they can identify with many of the objectives and methods of radical theologians.

Leaving aside the way 'radical' has come to be used in a political or religio-political sense, what exactly is its basic meaning? It is derived from the Latin 'radix', meaning a root. Radical is therefore 'going to the root or origin; touching or acting upon what is essential and fundamental; thorough' (Oxford Dictionary). It is also 'marked by a considerable departure from the usual or traditional... disposed to make extreme changes in existing views, habits, conditions or institutions' (Webster's Dictionary).

Though we shall be drawing some instructive parallels from the political use of the word, it is in this basic, non-political sense that we shall be speaking of the radical Christian.

The True Radical

'At the heart of the human problem is the problem of the human heart,' and only the Christian gospel claims to touch that. Other religions and philosophies may try to ameliorate his condition, but they leave the root untouched. Only the gospel speaks in terms of giving man 'a new heart' and 'a new spirit'. The committed Christian is therefore the product of a radical response to a radical message. But this is only the beginning. 'As you received Christ Jesus as Lord, continue to live in him,'[1] writes Paul. In other words, continue as you began. That first radical step leads to a radical walk. The New Testament Christian is radical in his outlook and life-style.

God's thinking and ways are as far removed from ours as the heavens are from the earth. When we were converted much of our thinking went into reverse gear. Our outlook on a number of cardinal issues is now the reverse of what it was before. Some things that we once loved we now hate, and some things that we hated we now love. When God converts a man he turns him upside down in order to get him right way up. This means that things that were formerly at the bottom go to the top, and others that were at the top go to the bottom. But God intends that this sudden reversal of thinking will lead to a process in which we are transformed by the renewing of our minds. 'Then you will be able to test and approve what God's will is—his good, pleasing and perfect will.'[2]

So the message of this book is a simple one. It involves the following propositions:

The God of the Bible is radical in all his dealings with men.

This fact was most clearly and powerfully demonstrated
in the life and ministry of his Son, Jesus Christ.
The kingdom of God is therefore utterly radical in its
demands.

If any man professes to call himself a child of God, a
disciple of Christ, or a citizen of the kingdom, and yet is
bereft of this radicalism, he would be well-advised to take
a long hard look at his Christian profession. Can it be real
gold without this hallmark?

A true radical of the kingdom is a man who stands on
clear ground in relation to truth. He cannot compromise
his conscience, tamper with his convictions, or bend biblical principles for the sake of status or security. Though he
does not court unpopularity for its own sake, he is not
afraid of it if it comes. His concern is to obey God, and
leave the consequences with him. All forms of unreality
or pretence are an anathema to him. In words and actions
he is captive to principle rather than expedience. This
means that he will not hesitate to speak the truth in love
for fear of hurting someone's feelings. Nor is he happy to
ignore matters which need to be raised, in order to avoid
an unpleasant confrontation. In the kingdom of God
radicalism means unswerving righteousness.

The clarity and courage of the radical Christian enables
him to cut through the hypocrisy, unreality and trivia that
often conceal root issues, as Jesus did with the scribes and
Pharisees, and expose the truth for all to see. He has
learned to discern between human enthusiasm and the zeal
of the Spirit, between soft-heartedness (which is basically
selfish) and spiritual compassion (which is sacrificial),
between easy-going tolerance and true forbearance. On
the other side of the coin, he is not stampeded into compromise for fear of people viewing him as narrow-minded,
exclusive, unco-operative, or superior.

In his convictions the radical is a black-and-white man.
Greys don't figure in his colour scheme. Or to put it

differently, when it comes to important issues he refuses to sit on the fence or adopt a 'wait-and-see policy'. It's right or it's wrong. It's true or it's false. It's light or it's darkness. He cannot go along with those who, for personal considerations, are content to live in the twilight.

The Man's a Fanatic

In the secular world men recognize that the radical is an enthusiast for his cause. He is thorough, whole-hearted. That's what they mean when they call him a fanatic. There is more than a pinch of truth in the assertion that 'when you call a Christian a fanatic you really mean that he loves Jesus more than you do!' Yes of course the radical Christian is a fanatic—in the way that Jesus was, and Paul. And—if one may be so bold—in the way that all too many professing Christians are not, but ought to be. He is not a special Christian. He simply qualifies for New Testament normality.

The radical Christian is naïve enough to think that his Lord and Master meant what he said when he declared that unless a man hated father, mother, wife, children, brothers, sisters, and his own life also—unless he shouldered his cross and followed him—unless he gave up everything he had, he would never be his disciple. That if his right eye was a hindrance he was to pluck it out, or if it was his right hand he was to amputate it. Does any communist manifesto contain anything more radical?

All too frequently, after the divine seed has germinated in a man's heart—after he has entered the kingdom by the strait gate and commenced to walk the narrow way—the radicalizing process slows down and eventually is arrested. He begins to revert to his old way of thinking. After all, it is far less demanding, and looking around it seems to him that most Christians have levelled off in a similar manner, and that of course eases his conscience. Ceasing to swim upstream he starts to drift with the current, or to swim just enough to stay where he is, and so avoid the epithet 'backslider'. For all that, he *is* a backslider. He has ceased to be an asset to the kingdom of God, and has become a liability.

The loss of true radicalism has leavened christendom with unreality, hypocrisy and compromise. The Christ of the Laodicean church thunders his warning at the close of this twentieth century just as he did at the close of the first. 'You're neither hot nor cold. Would to God you were one or the other. But this mixture of hot and cold, this luke-warmness makes me sick. Repent, before I vomit you out of my mouth.'[3] This is a call to New Testament radicalism. 'He who has an ear, let him hear what the Spirit says to the churches.'[4]

2

LET'S BEGIN WITH GOD

It was a Scottish castle in the Highlands where I and my family were staying as guests of a Christian lady who had just inherited the castle and the chieftainship of her clan. The place was full of historical interest, but what fascinated us most were the oil paintings of her ancestors, stretching back to the barons of medieval times. You could trace the family likeness over all those centuries, even to the present chief. How mysterious and how wonderful is the law of heredity.

John, in his first letter, possibly the most radical book in the whole of the Bible, makes it very clear that anyone who is born of God will display the Father's likeness. To claim to be a child of God and not show the family traits is to brand oneself an impostor.

In this chapter we shall see that God is radical in the true sense of the word. Before we can begin to talk about the radicalism of the Christian we must be absolutely clear that we are dealing with qualities that find their origin in God. By the same token we shall rule out of our discussion any aspects of 'radicalism' which are foreign to God's nature. Obviously one cannot deal with every aspect, but simply establish a solid base for all that follows. We are not dealing with etceteras but with essentials when we

18

touch the character of God.

'God is light; in him there is no darkness at all,'[1] says John. Imagine trying to explain to a man who had been born in some dark subterranean cavern, and had never seen the light of day, what the full blaze of the sun was like. Equally impossible is it for the natural mind to comprehend the blazing light of God's purity. 'God is a sun,' but without a single sun-spot. In action and reaction, in word and deed, in thought and motive he is without the slightest taint or trace of sin. He was and is and ever will be infinitely holy. In majestic words Paul describes him: 'God, the blessed and only Ruler, the King of kings and Lord of lords, who alone is immortal and who lives in unapproachable light, whom no-one has seen or can see.'[2]

God Is Angry

Before we condemn out of hand the anger and intolerance of the young radical, let us be honest enough to admit, however wrongly it may be expressed, that he is motivated by higher aspirations than the 'I'm all right Jack' philosophy of many of his contemporaries. He is angry at what he feels is the callous indifference of the privileged, or at the hypocritical arguments used to defend the status quo.

The political radical has his own lofty ideals and his own standards of justice, and he reacts accordingly. Of course to compare them with God's standards is like putting our grubby bed linen on a carpet of freshly fallen snow. But let us not miss the principle. Anger and intolerance is the inevitable reaction of a holy God towards all that contravenes that holiness. In this primary sense God is radical.

We have all heard sermons on God's love, but how many of us have heard anyone preach on his wrath? Yet the Bible writers have more to say about his anger than his love, and they do so without any apparent embarrassment, or any attempt to explain or justify it. 'Well, I suppose we should include it in the gospel to the sinner,' someone will say. But before we shrug it off as inapplicable to us, we should note that God's 'fierce anger' in the Old Testament is usually directed towards his own people, rather than the heathen.

Even the behaviour of Moses at the burning bush caused the Lord's anger to be kindled against him—and Moses was a man of God. It is the same in the New Testament. The letter to the Hebrews is addressed to 'holy brothers who share in the heavenly calling', and to them is the warning of chapter 10:

> If we deliberately keep on sinning after we have received the knowledge of the truth, no sacrifice for sins is left, but only a fearful expectation of judgment.... For we know him who said, 'It is mine to avenge; I will repay,' and again, 'The Lord will judge his people.' It is a dreadful thing to fall into the hands of the living God.[3]

Is this emphasizing only one side of God's character? Yes, the side which is all too often completely ignored. We need to restore the balance. Before we look at the other side, let us expose our minds and hearts to this radical edge of God's character. We need the Spirit of God to put that same edge on our characters too.

Anger versus Tolerance

Some of us have difficulty in reconciling anger with holiness. We equate anger with loss of temper, a vindictive spirit and other ungodly manifestations. 'God's wrath,' says J. I. Packer, 'is never the capricious, self-indulgent, irritable, morally ignoble thing that human anger so often is.... God is only angry when anger is called for.'[4] In fact, God's anger is as pure as his love, and the one does not contradict the other. R. A. Torrey went so far as to say that 'God's love to sinners will never be appreciated until seen in the light of his blazing wrath at sin'.[5]

If a Christian shares God's radicalism it is not that there will be times when he *may* be angry, but when he *must* be angry, when he will share God's righteous anger. 'In your anger do not sin,' says the Bible. That means there must be justification for our anger. And then it adds, 'Do not let the sun go down while you are still angry.'[6] In other words, get it off your chest, don't nurse it. Anger is never to be a safety valve for our uncontrollable irritation, or because we cannot have our own way, or even because we have been hurt or wronged. It must only be a response to a flagrant act of unrighteousness, something which is an offence to God.

Tolerance That Is Weak and Sickly

One reason why many of us shrink back from any serious consideration of righteous anger is that nowadays society in general and religious circles in particular have tended to treat *tolerance* as though it were almost the cardinal virtue before which every other righteous principle must give way. We must not confuse that fruit of the Spirit called patience, or the grace of forbearance, with a weak and sickly tolerance, advocated by those who are lenient towards themselves, and want everyone elso to act towards them in the same way.

The following lines, attributed to Robbie Burns, the Scottish poet, express the current thinking of man:

> There is so much good in the worst of us,
>   And so much bad in the best of us,
> That it ill behoves any of us
>   To criticise the rest of us.

That leaves us all in a cosy place of complacency, beyond the reach of the rebuke or correction of our fellows. Such sentiments have no place in God's thinking, and should have no place in ours.

There was a kindly man with a sympathetic ear, and the people in the church tended to go to him to pour out their tales of woe. His kindliness, however, was not laced with divine radicalism, with the result that many came to 'drip' on him their criticisms and resentments towards others in the church, even those in leadership. Though he knew that this was wrong he never spoke out against it, so people got the impression that he went along with what they were saying. He was not being 'salt' for God, and his lack of godly reaction gave opportunity to Satan, and in the end the brother himself became adversely affected.

Of course, where we are called to share God's intolerance, we must be continually on our guard against self-righteousness and hypocrisy. The tendency to judge our brother when we are guilty of the same fault is still with us. Our Lord warned us not to try to remove the speck of dust in our brother's eye until we had first removed the plank of wood from our own.[7]

The Virtue of Intolerance

The first thing we learn about God's moral character when we open our Bibles is that he is intolerant of mixture. We are presented with a world created by God and yet, for some undisclosed reason, in a state of chaos and confusion. At once God set to work to separate what was distinct and different, such as the light from the darkness. How creation got into its state of mixture need not concern us for the moment. The theologians are still arguing about it. It is much more important to grasp the spiritual lesson, that mixture must be sorted out if God's purpose for his creation is to be fulfilled.

The same principle was enshrined in the Mosaic law. For example, an Israelite was not to 'plough with an ox and a donkey yoked together'.[8] Paul used this to prohibit what has come to be called 'the unequal yoke', that is, a believer joining himself to an unbeliever, as in a marriage or business partnership.[9] God is equally intolerant of theological mixture, as with *syncretism*, or 'the attempt to blend opposite and contradictory tenets into one system to produce union and accord'. The end product is not the unity of the Spirit. At best it can only produce a blend of truth and error, of light and darkness, that leaves us in a murky twilight.

The kind of religious hotchpotch that goes by the name of the World Council of Churches, that seems to be based on discovering the lowest common denominator of truth that all those involved can agree upon, is equally an anathema to God. It smacks of an easy-going tolerance and of compromised convictions that are altogether foreign to the character of the God of truth.

Mixture in relation to church affiliation is a major cause of weakness in the body of Christ. Paul says, 'What fellowship can light have with darkness?[9] How then can a born-again minister be in harness with another who is manifestly unregenerate? Is not this 'the unequal yoke' in another form? Too many servants of God have allowed themselves to be manoeuvred by the enemy into the same kind of compromising alliance that marred the otherwise good reign of king Jehoshaphat. Time and again he dis-honoured God by aligning himself with the godless and idolatrous king of Israel. 'I will go with you,' he would say, 'I am as you are, my people as your people.'[10] What rubbish! His words were a betrayal of his standing as a servant of God. Little wonder the combined expeditions usually ended in near-disaster.

Local churches that are not based on the clear ground of personal commitment to Christ are another example of spiritual mixture, where those merely professing religion share membership with those who have the life of God.

Then there is the issue of righteousness. The radical Christian, because he is a child of God, will not be able to turn a blind eye or a deaf ear to that which does not measure up to the New Testament standard of righteousness, either in church or Christian organization, for fear of being accused of a 'holier-than-thou' attitude. He will stand to his convictions whatever the cost, and sometimes that cost is to 'come out from them and be separate'.[11]

Where Tolerance Is Sin

God, as we have seen, is always intolerant of sin, but there are certain sins which draw forth a much sharper reaction from him. When unrighteousnes or unreality find their way into the house of God, or defile those who are purporting to be his representatives, God is highly sensitive and shows himself utterly intolerant. The two sons of Eli the priest were evil men.[12] They treated the Lord's offering with contempt, and had promiscuous relationships with the women who served at the Tent of Meeting. Because Eli was in charge God held him responsible. He tried to reprove his sons, but they took no notice. He had left it much too late. Years of compromise had undermined his authority.

A man of God then came to Eli with a message from heaven. 'Why,' God asked, 'do you scorn my sacrifice and offering...? Why do you honour your sons more than me by fattening yourselves on the choice parts of every offering made by my people Israel?'[13] Notice, it was their profaning of God's house, not their immorality, that God highlighted. But the nub of the charge against Eli was of honouring his sons above God. He failed to restrain them because he feared them more than he feared the Lord.

God did not view the tolerance of Eli as weakness, but as sin, and all the more grievous because of his sacred position of privilege and trust. God reminded him of this:

Did I not clearly reveal myself to your father's house...? I chose your father out of all the tribes of Israel to be my priest, to go up to my altar, to burn incense, and to wear an ephod in my presence. I also gave your father's house all the offerings made with fire by the Israelites. Why do you scorn my sacrifice and offering...?[14]

Sin on the part of a spiritual leader, or the condoning of sin, is subject to severer penalty than the sin of one who does not have such responsibility. 'From everyone who has been given much, much will be demanded.'[15] The same principle lies behind James' warning: 'Not many of you should presume to be teachers, my brothers, because you know that we who teach will be judged more strictly.'[16]

God's final warning to Eli[17] only produced a passive and fatalistic response: 'He is the Lord; let him do what is good in his eyes.' Repentance and amendment could still have saved the day, but he was without a grain of radicalism in his system, and in the end judgement overtook him.

Hatred for Idolatry

God is radical in his relentless antipathy for every form of idolatry. When Israel was poised to enter the land of Canaan he told them: 'You must destroy all the peoples the Lord your God gives over to you. Do not look on them with pity and do not serve their gods, for that will be a snare to you.'[18] This seemingly ruthless policy was, firstly, the axe of divine judgement on nations whose iniquity had reached the point of no return;[19] and then it was to save Israel from being infected by this spiritual disease. The divine surgeon would use Israel as his knife to excise from the human race a cancer that threatened to destroy it. Surgery is radical treatment.

Anyone who thinks that God's extermination policy in Canaan was cruel and vindictive has never understood the nature of idolatry. We are not talking merely of forms and ceremonies, of shrines and images. Idolatry may be present where all these are absent. Even New Testament believers are warned to guard themselves from idols. Idolatry is a seductive thing which slowly and subtly entices the heart from God.

Holy Jealousy

As with Israel, ours is a covenant relationship with the Lord, and marriage is God's picture for it. In lifting up their voices against the nation's idolatry the prophets over and over again spoke of it in terms of violation of Israel's marriage covenant with Jehovah. It was marital infidelity.[20]

In the New Testament 'friendship with the world' is described as spiritual adultery.[21] This highlights another side of God's character. He is a jealous God, though there is nothing selfishly possessive about his love. John 3:16 tells us that. Any man who loves his wife deeply will inevitably be stirred by jealousy when he sees her falling for another lover. Anger, jealousy and intolerance will all compel him to act. Similarly God's jealousy means that he will brook no rival for our heart's affection. It is the depth of his love that guarantees the strength of his reaction when he sees 'the marriage' threatened.

God Unchanging

Many other aspects of God's radicalism will emerge as we proceed. Have you felt that the God of the Old Covenant is a God of fire and brimstone, while the God of the New is all love and grace? Good, I believe that too. But I also believe that the God of the Old Covenant is all love and grace, and the God of the New is fire and brimstone—especially in the book of Revelation! 'I the Lord do not change.'[22] As the old divines used to put it, God is immutable.

We may be certain that the God of the New Testament is no more and no less radical—no more and no less tolerant—than the God of the Old Testament. The Old Testament records that two priests, Nadab and Abihu, offered strange fire in the house of God, and were consumed. The New Testament records that two believer-priests, Ananias and Sapphira, committed an equivalent trespass, and also fell dead. It is not just the God of Sinai, but *our God* who *is a consuming fire.*[23] That sounds rather radical to me.

3

THE GREAT DIVIDE

While attending an English public school[1] Tony became a rebel against the conventional middle class society in which he was being reared, and eventually joined the Communist Party, until one day he found in Christ 'a radical alternative':

> By the age of 17 I had become an 'angry young man' who scorned religion, tradition and authority. Inwardly and—when I had the courage—outwardly I raged against the hypocrisy of the social order; against social gatherings where people were polite to one another's face, but tore each other apart behind their backs; against 'the rat race' and the all-important drive to accumulate wealth and prestige, which I could see did not give real happiness to anyone; against an empty religion where people prayed to God for his will to be done and then lived to please themselves; against the gulf between the rich and the poor.... I loved to ridicule the public school establishment and to deflate the pretensions of those who thought they were superior because of an accident of birth.

It was about the time of the great Vietnam demonstration in London in 1968 that Tony found himself being drawn increasingly to Marxist ideology, as a 'restless tide of revolutionary anger caught hold of young people all over the Western world'.

We saw pictures of students fighting the establishment in France, Germany, the United States, and imagined we were seeing the death agony of the decadent capitalist system in the world revolution which would bring in the new age of peace and socialism. In such a world God would have no place; and religion, like the other ideas that had bound and deceived mankind, would be thrown on to the rubbish heap of history. I began to feed my mind on Communist ideas and the undirected anger and resentment of my adolescence began to crystallise into a burning hatred of the capitalist system and a desire to see its end.

Tony was reading more and more Marxist literature. The hatred and violence that he found in the writings of Fanon and Guevara both drew him and scared him. In Guevara's *Venceremos* he read:

> Hatred is an element of the struggle, a relentless hatred of the enemy, impelling us over and beyond the natural limitations that man is heir to and transforming him into an effective, violent, selective and cold killing machine. Our soldiers must be thus. A people without hatred cannot vanquish a brutal enemy.

Marx versus Christ

It was in the course of an anti-Vietnam demonstration outside the USA Embassy in London that a girl thrust a leaflet into his hand. It contrasted the attitude to revolution of Marx with that of Christ. According to Marx the fault lay in the economic and political system. According to Jesus it lay within man's own nature. It is man who must be changed, liberated from his greed, selfishness and hatred by spiritual rebirth. Change the political system by revolution and the same evils will be produced under communism which existed under capitalism. Tony was coming to see this. Even the writings of some communists were confirming it. Mainly through the testimony and prayers of a Christian boy he had taught at school he found the answer in Christ. Subsequently he met the girl who had given him the tract. They are now married and being used together in God's service.

This testimony vividly illustrates the great divide between the revolutionary philosophy of the world, whether Left or Right, and that of the kingdom of God. The political radical is motivated by a spirit of hate, because either he has been a victim of injustice, or because, like Tony, his own sense of justice has been incensed by the façade that men have used to hide their own hypocrisy, and the arguments they have used to justify their own attitudes and actions. Witnessing 'man's inhumanity to man' tends to build up within a person an explosive mixture of anger, resentment, hatred and rebellion, and when numbers possessing a like spirit mingle it doesn't take much for the whole thing to erupt in violence.

The Right Balance

In the previous chapter we looked at the radical aspect of God's character. Now we must look at the other side. This is essential, not only to give us a balanced view of this theme, but also to help us to see with absolute clarity how man's radicalism at its very best is defiled and defiling, compared with the unsullied purity of that which comes from God.

We are told that 'God is love' and that 'God is light'. These are not contradictory but complementary facets. There is perfect light in God's love and perfect love in God's light. If we have not seen this our concept of God is faulty, and our vision of his character will be distorted. When Paul speaks of God's judgement on Israel for its unbelief, and of how the natural branches of 'the olive tree' were broken off that we Gentiles might be grafted in, he says: 'Consider therefore *the kindness and sternness of God*'.[2] To consider only his kindness without due regard to his sternness, as the moderns tend to do, is to leave us with an easy-going, indulgent God, whose response to man's sin is a pat on the head and a gentle 'Tut! tut!'. To consider only his sternness without consideration of his kindness is to be left with a fearsome God whose laws we obey only out of fear of 'the big stick'. Both of these are caricatures of the God and Father of our Lord Jesus Christ.

It should not be difficult to receive the chastisement of God when we see that it is an expression of his fatherly love, and with the purpose of conforming us to his likeness. 'The Lord disciplines those whom he loves, and he punishes everyone he accepts.'[3] Two small boys were up before their father for some serious misbehaviour. The penalty was a good spanking, but before administering the 'laying on of hands' he asked if they had anything to say. At this one of them bowed his head and solemnly repeated, 'For what we are about to receive may the Lord make us truly thankful'! He had reason indeed to be thankful that he had a father that loved him enough not to spare him pain to develop his character.

Reflected in Christ

Since Jesus was the perfect reflection of God it is not surprising that we see the same perfect balance in him. His tirade on the scribes and Pharisees in Matthew 23 contains the most scathing denunciations anywhere in Scripture, concluding with the terrible words, 'You snakes! You brood of vipers! How will you escape being condemned to hell?' But before the words are scarcely out of his mouth the tears are coursing down his cheeks as he utters the heart-breaking lament, 'O Jerusalem, Jerusalem, you who kill the prophets and stone those sent to you, how often I have longed to gather your children together, as a hen gathers her chicks under her wings, but you were not willing.'[4]

There is a place, as we have already said, for a clear and uncompromising declaration of the righteous demands of God. But let him beware who proclaims God's wrath without mercy in his heart and tenderness in his voice. A certain pastorate was vacant, and possible candidates were being invited to the church to preach. One man came and took the text, 'The wicked shall be turned into hell.' At the vestry meeting it was decided that he was not their man. Next Sunday another came and preached on the identical text and received a unanimous invitation to the pastorate. When someone remonstrated with the deacons for the inconsistency of their decision, they replied, 'The man we have invited to the pastorate preached on the text with tears in his eyes, but when the other man told us that the wicked would be turned into hell he seemed rather pleased about it.'

The one who will preside on that coming day of judgement, from whose presence earth and heaven will flee away, is none other than the meek and lowly Lamb of sacrifice, who offered himself for the sin of the world. It is to him who cried in his hour of agony 'Father, forgive them, they know not what they do' that all judgement has been committed. The book of Revelation pictures the great of the earth—kings, princes, generals, the rich and the mighty, the slave and the free—hiding in caves and among the rocks of the mountains, calling on the mountains and the rocks to fall on them and hide them 'from the face of him who sits on the throne and from the wrath of the Lamb!'[5] Here is the ultimate ordeal that unbelieving humanity will face—a wrath terrible because of its purity, mighty because of its meekness, devastating because of its tenderness: *the wrath of the Lamb*.

The Natural and the Spiritual

We have already made mention of some of the basic

ingredients of political radicalism. Let us now contrast them with the characteristics of that radicalism which comes from God. *Hatred*, as we have seen, is invariably the great driving force. It was not enough for Jesus merely to prohibit hate. He dealt with this deadly negative by declaring a glorious positive: '*Love* your enemies and pray for those who persecute you.'[6] And then he poured out God's love into the hearts of his disciples by the giving of his Holy Spirit to make it all come true. It was this that enabled Stephen to follow so closely the example of his master, for when they were stoning him to death he cried out, 'Lord, do not hold this sin against them.'[7]

As for *rebellion*, although there were revolutionary movements abroad in the days of Christ, he never associated with them. When men would come and take him by force to make him king, he shied away.[8] When his disciples informed him that certain Greeks wanted to see him, he never gave them an interview, but spoke instead of the necessity of the grain of wheat falling into the ground and dying.[9] Before Caiaphas Jesus remained silent until the high priest charged him under oath to say who he was. Only then did Jesus reply. It was an act of submission to the nation's ruler.[10] Similarly Paul, when he discovered that the one whom he had called 'a whitewashed wall' was the high priest, acknowledged publicly the scripture, 'Do not speak evil about the ruler of your people.'[11]

The New Testament writers speak with one voice on this matter of submission to the secular authority. We do not obey the authority because it is necessarily good, or right, or just. We obey it because it has been established by God. It is his delegated authority. 'He who rebels against the authority is rebelling against what God has instituted.... Give everyone what you owe him: If you owe taxes, pay taxes; if revenue, then revenue; if respect, then respect; if honour, then honour.'[12] This is a totally unacceptable principle to the secular radical or revolutionary, for it robs him of what he believes is his major weapon. The Revised Standard version of Proverbs 24:21 links obedience to the divine authority with obedience to the secular: 'My son, fear the Lord and the king, and do not disobey either of them;' or, as The Living Bible puts it, 'don't associate with radicals'!

Then rebellion tends to issue in *violence*. Protest, demonstration, political pressure are their first recourse. If these do not speedily accomplish their ends they resort to strong-arm tactics, if necessary the bullet and the bomb, to dictate their will. They are determined to bring about what the people need, even if it's not what the people want. And so tyranny is employed to overthrow tyranny.

Nothing could be further from the spirit by which Christ establishes his rule. 'My kingdom,' he told Pilate, 'is not of this world. If it were, my servants would fight to prevent my arrest by the Jews. But now my kingdom is from another place.'[13]

In *Saul the Pharisee* on the one hand, and *Paul the apostle* on the other, we see epitomized in one person both the secular and the Christian radical. The fanatical Pharisee is on his way to Damascus, breathing out threatenings and slaughter against the disciples of the Lord. Ananias is told to go and minister to him, but he is not at all enthusiastic, despite the assurances of the Lord. Now see those elders of the Ephesian church crowding round Paul the apostle, as he kneels down and prays with them all for the last time. They all weep as they embrace and kiss him, knowing that they are looking on the face of this rugged fearless apostle for the last time. Here is a radical of a different order.

Beware of the Carry Over

When we deal with the radical element in the kingdom of God we are touching high tension cables, and we need to know what we are doing. It is all too easy to carry over the spirit and the methods of the secular into the realm of the spiritual with disastrous results. These are often apparent when strong words or actions result in wounding instead of healing; driving apart instead of drawing together; and pulling down instead of building up.

It takes honesty, courage and humility to look frankly at the end-product in such cases and ask the question, 'Did we handle it aright?' The argument that the one at the receiving end was not submissive to authority may not be the whole truth, or even part of the truth. Sometimes the negative results are caused by a harsh and heavy-handed authority. Radical action may well have been called for, but what kind of action came through? Was it from heaven or from men?

It is *the Lamb* who has taken the spirit of the cross up to the throne. It is the Lamb on the throne that will one day sit in judgement. If meanwhile he permits his servants to exercise judgement in certain situations it must be with the lamb-like spirit. The lamb is the symbol of meekness, lowliness and sacrifice. Harshness and aggressiveness come from a spirit of pride. Correction of others, Paul tells us, is always to be performed not primarily by one who is strong, but by one who is 'spiritual'; not with an attitude of superiority but in 'a spirit of meekness'—the lamb-like spirit—and in humble watchfulness, knowing that he who corrects could be overtaken in the same fault.[14]

A critical spirit that tends to be destructive is another carry-over that we need to watch. There are those who are adept at pulling down, but poor at building up. They are skilled at snuffing out strange fire, but not at rekindling the true flame. They are quick to point out a brother's nakedness, but slow to cover it up. They are good at sniffing out every form of pseudo-spirituality, but not at cultivating true spirituality. Such radicalism is to be rejected because it has a selfish motivation.

Here is an acid test of spiritual authority in the kingdom of God. Does it smack of self-interest or of service? Does it minister to the ego of the one who exercises it, or serve the interests of the one over whom it is exercised? 'The kings of the Gentiles,' said Jesus to his apostles, 'lord it over them.... But *you are not to be like that.* Instead, the greatest among you should be like the youngest, and *the one who rules like the one who serves.'*[15] Let us read that again until the truth sinks in. The one who rules is to be like the one who serves. The true radical must know the touch of the cross upon his radicalism. Only this can give him a dedication to the good of others that is free from the taint of self-importance and self-interest.

The radical Christian is strong, but his toughness is mingled with tenderness, and his conviction with compassion. It is Luke who tells us that having wept over Jerusalem Jesus entered the temple and drove out the racketeers.[16] Has he a right to whip who has not first learned to weep? When the spirit of the Lamb permeates our radicalism its cutting edge will be sharpened, not blunted, and instead of leaving behind a trail of division and destruction it will leave behind 'a harvest of righteousness'.

4

TAKING ANOTHER LOOK

It was one of those popular artist's impressions of Christ that looked down at me from the wall of a friend's home. I have never been drawn to such pictures. No artist can portray our Lord's Godhood, only his humanity, so he only depicts one half of Christ. And since we know nothing of his human form any portrait of the human Jesus must be imaginary. I found it hard to reconcile this golden-haired Christ with the face of a Palestinian Jew. And surely the reason why the Bible tells us nothing about his human form is that knowing him 'after the flesh'[1] only hinders us knowing him in the Spirit.

Quite apart from these reasons I could not imagine that the human Jesus was really as this artist depicted him. Characterwise there was something missing. The kindliness and winsomeness were there, but not the resolution and the strength of character that marked the Son of man. So often these vital ingredients are omitted in our character studies of Christ. We have been taught about his meekness and gentleness, his humility and servanthood, his mercy and compassion, purity and holiness, even his faith and miracle-working power. But we have overlooked the revolutionary teacher, the controversialist, the provocative preacher, the man who disregarded convention and protocol, the implacable opponent of the religious establishment, the leader who associated with all the wrong types, and who seemed intent in provoking rather than placating his critics. In this chapter we shall look at the radical Christ.

A Disturbance at Court

Herod the Great was King of the Jews, though as an Edomite this was contrary to the law of Moses.[2] By currying the favour of the Roman Emperor he had gained the throne. Though an able and powerful ruler his deeply suspicious nature had resulted in several murderous outbursts whenever he suspected his throne was threatened. When some eminent yet mysterious visitors from the east arrived at Herod's court enquiring after the newly born 'King of the Jews', Herod, his courtiers and the whole of Jerusalem were filled with alarm.

A baby born in a stable of lowly Hebrew stock! A child without money, position or influence! One who would never live to wield a sword or marshal an army! Whatever had kings and the great of the earth to fear from a birth so insignificant? Far more than they could ever have realized! Herod would surely have suffered an attack of apoplexy had he known that this child was destined by the decree of the Most High to overthrow the throne of kingdoms and to inherit the nations of the earth.

Herod would have been shocked to know that this mysterious babe of Bethlehem was to be the embodiment of that stone 'cut out by no human hand' that was destined to smite 'the great image' (man's world empire) and make the kingdoms of earth like the chaff of the summer threshing floors.[3] Within a generation God would set him as King on Zion's holy hill and give to him dominion, glory and a kingdom, that all peoples, nations and languages should serve him.

It should be no surprise that the birth of this revolutionary world-ruler created such an alarm in the ruling echelons of society. The satanically inspired attempt on his life that followed reflected the spiritual disturbance taking place among the powers of darkness. Though his contemporaries did not recognize him as the coming world-ruler, nor even as the Messiah of Israel, all undoubtedly recognized him as a radical and a revolutionary. For us the passage of the centuries and the familiarity of the gospel story have blurred this image.

The Marks of a Radical

A people bored to tears with the platitudes of the scribes gasped in astonishment at the revolutionary teaching that fell from the lips of the prophet of Nazareth. But it wasn't simply his teaching; his life-style was wholly in keeping with what he taught. In stark contrast with the prevailing religious fashion, he focused on men's inward rather than their outward state. He was primarily concerned with heart condition, with attitude and motive. And like all radicals, he was wholly intolerant of unreality and hypocrisy.

His values were diametrically opposed to those of the money-loving Pharisees. With him all material interests were subordinate to the supreme interests of the heavenly kingdom. His zeal was red hot whenever the honour of his Father was at stake. He burned with indignation when he found hucksters and tricksters in his Father's house making a mint at the expense of the worshippers. He kicked over the tables of the money changers, scattering their change in all directions, and with a whip of small cords drove them from the sanctuary.

We shall see how his behaviour towards his human family seemed at times out of character. He did not hesitate to disregard convention if it stood between him and the will of God, and religious traditions he simply ignored.

With regard to his handling of men, whether it was his own disciples or others who came to him, his discernment and counsel always penetrated with unerring accuracy to the root issue.

Christ's radicalism stands out in sharpest relief when we find him in a confrontation with the religious leaders. At times his words and actions were intentionally provocative, as though he was determined to bring issues to the surface, and he did not hesitate to use the most scathing language to denounce their hypocrisy. Bad characters and social outcasts, however, were irresistibly drawn to his circle. All this was further fuel for his critics—'Birds of a feather' would have been their jibe. The poor and the despised were the ones who hung on his words, while the traditionalists and the religionists hurried away, inwardly fuming, to plot how they might silence him for ever.

Let us now look at some of these aspects in greater detail.

Family Relationships

As children we may have been taught about the beautiful submission of Jesus to his parents during those formative years of his life in the Nazareth homestead. Then, when his life was ebbing away, he took thought for that widowed mother, committing her to the tender care of the disciple he loved. But there were other occasions when his behaviour towards his earthly family is inexplicable, unless we bear in mind this radical element of his character.

His parents had taken their twelve-year-old up to Jerusalem for the Feast of the Passover. On the return journey they discovered he was missing. Three days later they found him in the temple with a captive audience of learned theologians. Was he not old enough to realize that to go missing in this way would have his parents stiff with worry? One feels some sympathy with Mary's scolding question, 'Son, why have you treated us like this? Your father and I have been anxiously searching for you.'

The boy's answer was profound, almost prophetic, for it set forth what was to be for him a life principle: 'Did you not know that I must be busy with my Father's affairs?'[4] That devoted mother, who at his birth had 'pondered in her heart' the sayings of the shepherds, had now something more to ponder.

When the wine ran out at the wedding in Cana of Galilee Mary must have felt for the family that was responsible. It was a situation of acute embarrassment. 'They have no more wine,' she whispered to her son, with the implied suggestion that he should now start to use that miraculous power she knew he possessed to do something about it. His response: 'O woman, what have you to do with me? My hour has not come.'[5] Though his reply was not impolite in that Jewish culture, why this gentle reproof?

The Relationship Had Changed

His mission had just begun. His first miracle had not yet been performed. Mary was right. This *was* the occasion for it. But she must understand that their relationship had now changed. The initiation and timing of this event must be at the prompting of the Spirit that now rested upon him. Highly favoured though Mary was, she had to learn that in matters affecting his ministry he could only move at his Father's bidding, and their special human relationship must now fade into the background. This lesson was reinforced by a later incident.

It was a packed house meeting that Jesus was addressing when he received a message that his mother and brothers were outside wanting to see him. It was a request that called on him to drop what he was doing. '"Who are my mother and my brothers?" he asked. Then he looked at those seated in a circle around him and said, "Here are my mother and my brothers! Whoever does God's will is my brother and sister and mother.'"[6]

The claims of his family versus the claims of his ministry was the issue. He must give priority to the spiritual relationship over against the natural. This principle he later summarized in one of the most radical statements that he ever uttered. 'If anyone comes to me and does not hate his father and mother, his wife and children, his brothers and sisters—yes, even his own life—he cannot be my disciple.'[7] On another occasion, when a man expressed his willingness to follow Jesus, provided he could be allowed first to say goodbye to his family, he was told, 'No-one who puts his hand to the plough and looks back is fit for service in the kingdom of God.'[8] When it comes to human relationships the divine claims must reign supreme. Jesus not only taught it. He practised it.

The Touch of the Cross

Have no fear that this radical element that we see in our Lord's human relationships will result in families being neglected for the sake of God's kingdom. Wherever this happens it is because of a misunderstanding and a misapplication of what Jesus taught. He himself gives us the key to this riddle of *hating* when he goes on to speak of hating 'one's own life also'. This means carrying our cross, as the context here and elsewhere shows.[9]

A man hates his own life when he is willing to embrace the cross by becoming the kernel of wheat that falls to the ground and dies.[10] A man hates father and mother, wife and children when he is willing for the cross to touch those human relationships. Did any man ever injure his own spiritual life by embracing the cross? Why then should we think that the same principle operating in our family relationships would injure those we love? The cross may often bring hurt but it will never bring harm.

To be soft-hearted, sentimental and indulgent towards those we love means that we are more concerned about pleasing them than pleasing God. This, not the other, is the attitude that causes spiritual injury. When the cross comes into our relationships we are ready for sacrifice and suffering, for separation and self-denial, should the will of God require it, but the result will always be blessing. Look at Abraham. The principle of the cross in human relationships was the great lesson he had to learn all through his life, until at last he was willing to lay even his Isaac on the altar. And that was the best thing he ever did, for Isaac as well as for himself.

Dealing with the Roots

Let us now move from the area of human relationships and consider our Lord's handling of individuals who came to him. In this he was not only masterly, he was radical. Why did he not tell the rich young ruler to *tithe* his possessions and give that to the poor?[11] Or would it not have been enough to persuade him to imitate the wealthy Zacchaeus and give away *half* of his goods? No, Jesus told him to sell *all* and give away *all*. Why? His problem was not that he possessed great wealth, but that his great wealth possessed him. The eye of the surgeon had diagnosed a cancer called 'the love of money', and radical surgery was the only hope.

There was the paralysed man let down through the roof by his four friends.[12] How easy it would have been to speak the word of healing or to touch that suffering body as he had touched countless others. But no, he looked beyond the sick body to the sick heart. It could have been that Jesus had discerned that the two were connected, or as we say today, that his disease was psychosomatic. In any case he saw that the man's greater need was forgiveness, not healing, so he pronounced forgiveness, and then healed him to prove that the forgiveness was real.

How often Jesus probed his way into the thoughts and intents of a man's heart by means of one carefully chosen question. 'Do you want to get well?'[13] must have sounded strange to the ears of a chronic invalid! Didn't Jesus know that that was just what he had been wanting for thirty-eight years? Each day as he lay by the Pool of Bethesda he spent his time hoping, hoping, hoping. But had he faced up to all the implications?

To be rid of the pain, the weakness, the humiliation, that would be great. But what about being rehabilitated after all these years? What about finding a job, starting to pay his way, to support his family, instead of being an object of charity? What about the mending of broken relationships? Most important of all, was he ready to break with the sin that had brought it all upon him? Men may want salvation, deliverance, healing, or the filling of the Spirit, but unless they are willing for a change in their way of life there will be no permanent work. 'Sin no more, that nothing worse befall you,' were Jesus' last words to this man.

Testing Faith to the Limit

Sometimes Jesus treated men in what we might think was an off-hand, even discourteous way, but always there was a valid spiritual reason. There was the royal official who came to plead with Jesus to accompany him to Capernaum and heal his son who was desperately sick.[14] 'Unless you people see miraculous signs and wonders...you will never believe,' was Jesus' seemingly unfeeling response. 'Sir, come down before my child dies,' cried the man in desperation. Only then did Jesus speak the life-giving word, 'You may go. Your son will live.'

Jesus' tactics were similar with the Canaanite woman whose demonized daughter was suffering grievously.[15] At first Jesus did not answer her at all. Thinking that he did not want to bother with her the disciples urged him to send her away. But Jesus answered, 'I was sent only to the lost sheep of Israel.' At this the woman came and knelt before him pleading for help. Surely now he would respond, but still he held back. 'It is not right to take the children's bread and toss it to their dogs,' he replied. It is hard to think of anything more provocative for a Jew to say to a Gentile, but it drew from this woman one of the greatest expressions of faith to be found in the gospels: 'Even the dogs eat the crumbs that fall from the masters' table,' she replied. Jesus could hold back no longer. 'Woman, you have great faith! Your request is granted.'

Our Lord's radical approach is urgently needed today in the counselling room, whether dealing with those seeking salvation or those looking for answers to spiritual problems. We live in a world that demands 'instant everything'. There is always the pressure to produce results, to chalk up another 'success'. The counsellor is therefore tempted to make it as easy as possible for those being counselled to make the right responses or the right decisions. Jesus, on the other hand, often made it as difficult as possible.

We must learn from 'the wonderful Counsellor' that 'success' is not the name of the exercise. Too many of our 'success' cases prove to be ultimate failures. Jesus himself didn't always achieve 'success' as men define it. There was one point where he suffered a mass defection of disciples.[16] But he always touched the root of the matter and compelled men to face reality. The radical approach will mean that we shall not always be able to report, 'He came right through.' Sometimes it may have to be, 'He went away sorrowful,' but always there will be the assurance that the word of God has been spoken and the judgement of God has been brought.

Training Disciples in Faith

Our Lord knew that it would take radical treatment to make those rough-hewn characters men of faith, but he was determined to do so. With this in view he put them through a rugged training course. Again and again they were 'thrown in the deep end' as he involved them in his own miraculous ministry, the feeding of the four thousand and the five thousand, the walking on the water, the tribute money from the fish's mouth, the two miraculous catches of fish, and of course his sending them forth to drive out evil spirits and heal every kind of sickness and disease. Again and again he rebuked them sharply when faith did not rise to the occasion.

They were on the Sea of Galilee that they knew so well.[17] 'A furious squall came up, and the waves broke over the boat, so that it was nearly swamped.' They had faced storms before, but this was something else. For once those hardened and experienced fishermen took up panic stations, convinced that their last moment had come.

It was true that Christ was on board, but you wouldn't have thought so by the reaction of these disciples—in the same way that no one would think that we had him on board when we panic in our emergencies! So relaxed was Christ that he had fallen asleep despite the storm. 'Lord, save us! We're going to drown!' they cried. With majestic poise he rose and spoke peace to the raging waters. Then he turned his attention to the trembling disciples. Surely they needed calming, comforting and reassuring. But listen to his words: 'You of little faith, why are you so afraid?'

No Excuses Allowed

When Jesus came down from the mount of Transfiguration he found a demonized boy, a shame-faced bunch of disciples, and a gesticulating father trying to explain that these followers of his had failed to heal his son.[18] In the past they had achieved great success in dealing with evil spirits, so this must have been a humiliating experience for them. 'I'm sorry you didn't succeed, but you did your best' was not how Jesus responded to their failure. He issued a rebuke before that watching, listening crowd that must have made those disciples feel about as tall as Tom Thumb! 'O unbelieving and perverse generation, how long shall I stay with you? How long shall I put up with you? Bring the boy here to me.' And then to crown their humiliation he drove out the demon with a word.

Similar was the occasion when Peter, responding to the word of Jesus, began to imitate his Master by walking on the water. Remember, the disciples had not yet received the Holy Spirit. They were not yet fully moving in the supernatural as they were to do after Pentecost. Yet here was Peter doing what no other had ever done, apart from Christ. Then came the attack of fear, the 'sinking feeling' and the cry for help to which Jesus instantly responded. 'Never mind, Peter, you did actually walk on the water. Marvellous! Those other disciples wouldn't dare.' Peter didn't get off so lightly. 'You of little faith,' said Jesus, 'why did you doubt?'[19]

Unbelief Is Always Blameworthy

When Jesus met with his disciples in resurrection we learn that 'he *rebuked* them', and the word used here is very strong indeed, rendered *upbraided* in our older versions, 'for their lack of faith and their stubborn refusal to believe those who had seen him after he had risen.'[20] Frequently, especially in the closing days of his earthly ministry, Jesus had forewarned his disciples of his impending death, and given them the promise of his rising again. Their failure to believe was therefore inexcusable, and his rebuke correspondingly severe.

If it seems to us that at times Jesus was a little hard with his disciples we have only to look ahead into the Acts to see what men of faith they became. In *The Fourth Dimension* Paul Yonggi Cho of Korea shares with us how he became a man of faith. God does not seem to have made the training course in faith any easier for twentieth-century saints. We need to be tough with ourselves, and if we have responsibility for training others, we must be tough with them if ever we are to see a generation arise who will really believe God.

Conformist or Non-Conformist?

Here for the moment we must leave uncompleted our pen portrait of the radical Christ, though we shall return to it again. Enough has been said to establish that in this, as in every other respect, Jesus was 'the express image' of his heavenly Father.

Face to face with the radical Christ we have to ask ourselves whether we are yet '*conformed* to the likeness of [God's] Son'.[21] 'Am I a conformist or a non-conformist?' If we find ourselves weighed in the balance and found wanting, let us remember that God has sent forth the Spirit of his Son into our hearts to reproduce in us the likeness of Jesus. Let us call on God to make us just as radical as his Son in every area of our lives. And then trust him to do it.

5

THE NARROW GATE

Special Air Services is a Commando-type outfit that
operates under a cloak of secrecy. Very little was known
about them until they carried out the successful raid on
the Iranian embassy in London, and rescued the embassy
hostages held by terrorists. At that time a few facts were
released. The SAS is apparently composed of specially
selected, highly trained men, all of whom are volunteers.
In keeping with the nature of the service, the terms of
entry are tough. On average only one out of every five is
accepted. It is like this with the kingdom of God. The
terms of entry are as radical as the kingdom itself.

Anciently the Greek mysteries required their initiates
to go through certain purification rites and other disciplines
before they could be received and enjoy the privileges of
the new society. In the same way there is *a path of initiation*
that the would-be-disciple of the kingdom must tread if he
would enjoy the full benefits of the heavenly society.
Jesus made it clear that 'the gate is narrow and the way is
hard, that leads to life'.[1] But over the years men have
removed the gates, knocked down the gate-posts, and
generally widened the gateway so as to make it easy for all
and sundry to enter. Inevitably standards have been
lowered, spirituality watered down, and the sharp edge of

testimony blunted. Nowadays the professing church is 'a mixed multitude', far removed from the first Christian community, of whom we read, 'No-one else dared join them, even though they were highly regarded by the people.'[2] To belong to 'that lot' you had to be real. It was 'all or nothing'. The professing church will never again be a radical society until its radical terms of entry are observed, as they were in the early church.

To ascertain what those terms of entry really are we do well to avoid the perilous rapids of ecclesiastical tradition and church history and trace the river back to its source. The day of Pentecost saw the first huge intake. But what were the terms? In response to the anguished appeal of the crowds, 'Brothers, what shall we do?', Peter gave the simple, clear, uncompromising answer, 'Repent and be baptized, every one of you, in the name of Jesus Christ, so that your sins may be forgiven. And you will receive the gift of the Holy Spirit.' In what has been sometimes dubbed 'the Peter package' we have three elements—*repentance*, the key to the new birth; *water baptism*, by which men are required to seal that step; and *the gift of the Holy Spirit*, by which it is sealed by God. In this chapter we shall deal with the first of these.

No Substitutes Allowed

In striking contrast to humanistic and evolutionary theories of man being able to lift himself up by his boot straps to loftier moral and social heights, the gospel cuts the ground from beneath his feet. It calls on him to repent, that is, to admit to his own defeat and failure, to his moral and spiritual bankruptcy. The gospel declares that man's hope is not to be found in evolution but in *revolution*—revolution that is inward and spiritual. *Repent* is the first word of the gospel. It was the first word on the lips of John the Baptist, of Jesus, of the apostles, of the early church. There is no word in the whole of the gospel more radical, for it lays the axe to the root of all that man is in himself. It sounds the death knell to all humanistic pretensions, for it says in effect, 'Man, you cannot make it.'

No human substitutes such as religion, morality, reformation, or respectability will ever be accepted by God in place of repentance. It signifies so much more than simply being sorry, more even than remorse, which may be nothing more than self-pity. Repentance is a full-blooded, whole-hearted, uncompromising renunciation of one's former attitude and outlook. It is a change of heart that always results in a change of course—what John the Baptist called 'fruit in keeping with repentance'.[3] The fruit may be summarized in one word—*conversion,* the act of turning round and facing in the opposite direction.

The true disciple is not only one in whose heart this foundation has been well laid, but one who seeks to lay that foundation in the lives of those whom he in turn is called to disciple. We have just seen how Jesus did this. Again and again in such a simple and yet masterly way he pinpointed the crucial issue between the individual and God.

With the woman of Samaria it was an issue of moral laxity, and his word, 'Go, call your husband and come back,'[4] led to the whole issue coming out into the light. With the man at the Pool of Bethesda it was the challenge of whether he was willing to be made whole, and that meant, as the sequel showed, to 'stop sinning'.[5] With the rich young ruler Jesus fastened on his love of riches, and demanded that he sell all and give to the poor—that was radical enough—and then follow Christ.[6] Nicodemus, on the other hand, who was a theologian and a teacher, was told in effect that all his religious knowledge could not avail. He needed to humble himself and become as a little child. He needed to be born again.[7] Zacchaeus' salvation turned on the issue of his submission to Christ's authority when Jesus had taken the liberty of inviting himself to tea.

His readiness to make restitution to any he had wronged followed naturally from this.[8]

Guilty Preachers

Far too many are slipping into the kingdom without coming through the narrow gate of repentance. Little wonder so many are sickly babes instead of robust disciples. Little wonder that so many never seem to get beyond the stage of needing counselling, deliverance, or emotional healing. No wonder so many always have to be carried and never reach the place where they can begin to carry others. This is not an indictment of weak believers so much as an indictment of those who preach a deficient gospel, and press people into a premature commitment to Christ before the Holy Spirit has done a thorough work of conviction. Something vital is lost when we pick the fruit before it is ripe. It was said that William Carey, the pioneer missionary to India, was 'slow to accept a profession of Christianity even though the sacrifice involved was often great. "Let nothing short of a *radical change of heart* satisfy you in your converts" was one of his sayings.'[9]

The gospel is free, thank God, but that does not mean it is 'cheap and easy', yet all too often that is the kind of gospel that has been presented. The great publicity that attends modern evangelism, the tendency to count heads and advertise conversion statistics, puts great pressure on evangelists to produce results at all costs. And since the evangelist is looked upon as the expert, he consciously or unconsciously sets the standard for everyone else down the line, so that even the personal counsellor is eager to chalk up his success. It is short-sighted as well as unbiblical to make it too easy for the seeker to get in.

'Will I have to give up my smoking and drinking?' was the anxious question of a young man seeking salvation. 'Yes, you will,' was the uncompromising answer. 'But giving up smoking and drinking is not a scriptural condition of salvation,' someone will say. True, but nor is selling all you have and giving to the poor, yet when the Holy Spirit pinpoints an issue, *that issue* becomes the battleground on which a man will either yield or resist, receive Christ or reject him. We are not helping but hindering the work of the Spirit by trying to shift the fighting on to what we consider is a more scriptural battlefield. Don't try to be wiser than the Holy Spirit. It is a most unproductive exercise.

Keep Conversion Big

In many historic churches where the message of 'renewal' has come there has been a tendency to play down or overlook the new-birth experience. This is particularly the case in churches where there has never been a strong evangelistic emphasis. The new birth is absolutely fundamental. It is illogical to invite people who have never possessed life to be revived, and those who have never been 'born' to be renewed. People who are religious but unregenerate need to hear the word 'repent' as much as the godless and the irreligious. There is a 'repentance from dead works', and all religion devoid of spiritual life comes into this category. There is many a Nicodemus in the pew as well as the pulpit whose 'religion' has become a barrier between him and God, and who needs to be told, 'You must be born again.'

The experience of the new birth is more fundamental, more radical than that of receiving the Spirit. It is described as coming out of darkness into light, as passing from death to life, as being delivered from the dominion of Satan and translated into the kingdom of God's dear Son, as becoming a new creation in Christ, as old things passing away and all things becoming new. It must be supreme in our thinking and in our preaching of the good news of the kingdom. The offer of salvation is God's offer to the sinner, but the gift of the Spirit is the Father's promise to his child,[10] and you need to be his child to qualify. Jesus' own words made this clear: 'How much more will *your Father* in heaven give the Holy Spirit to those who ask him!'[11] Unless we thoroughly lay the foundation stone of repentance in the lives of those we disciple for the kingdom, we are building on sand.

6

THE CLEAN BREAK

If repentance is entering the narrow gate, then water baptism is the gate clanging shut behind you. Baptism doesn't get you in, but once you have entered by repentance and faith, baptism seals you in. It is a sign to the believer that in his committal to Christ he has taken a step that is decisive and irrevocable. In their deliverance from Egypt the Israelites were 'baptised into Moses...in the sea.'[1] In other words, they were united with Moses as their deliverer and head in a symbolic baptism when they passed through the Red Sea. It typifies our union with Christ in the rite of baptism. When the Israelites had passed through the sea the waters rolled back and engulfed their pursuers. By that one decisive act of baptism in the sea they were cut off from Egypt and all that it stood for—and cut off for ever. Baptism signifies *a clean break from the old life*.

An Issue of Conflict

I first met Brother Andrew, 'God's Smuggler', in the London headquarters of the newly formed Fountain Trust. Those were the very early days of the charismatic movement, and there was much excitement at what God was doing in the churches through the baptism of the Holy Spirit, despite opposition. I recall my surprise when our Dutch brother remarked that the major issue of conflict would prove to be over *water baptism*, not the baptism in the Spirit. The intervening years have certainly proved that people are generally brought more easily to a change of stance over Spirit baptism than water baptism. This could be because water baptism is all too often viewed as a denominational issue, and so becomes a question of denominational loyalty. Sometimes the defence of infant baptism is a defence of ecclesiastical or ministerial authority. But there may be deeper reasons.

Many of us who are committed to the Spirit's work of restoration in the church are more than ever convinced of the great importance of this ordinance. The New Testament practice of immersing in water new converts in Christ does something significant for the convert. It does something significant for the body of believers to whom he is being added. It does something to the watching world. Perhaps most important of all, it does something to the principalities and powers in the heavenly places. If it involves contention in the heavens little wonder it evokes some controversy on earth. Where the gospel is being preached to heathen communities, as foreign missionaries will vouch, it is not the act of receiving Christ on the part of say, a Hindu or a Muslim—not even his public confession of Christ—but his baptism in water that seems to stir up persecution. The adversary is evidently strongly antagonistic to the baptism of believers.

An Intolerant Attitude

A letter just published in a Christian magazine pleaded for a tolerant attitude over matters in which there was a difference of opinion among Christians. Mention was made of 'the Christian who insists on adult baptism with total immersion, and says any other type of baptism is completely invalid'. Let us be clear, there is no plea here for *adult baptism* as such. As F. B. Meyer used to say, 'A man may be as old as Methuselah and still not qualify for baptism.' It is not a question of age, but of faith. It is *believers' baptism* that we are advocating.

However strongly one holds to believers' baptism there should always be tolerance towards those who hold firmly and sincerely to a paedobaptist position, and who genuinely cannot see why we make 'all this fuss about believers' baptism'. But you cannot be tolerant towards the practice itself since it is both erroneous and harmful. Nor can you be tolerant towards those who continue to practise it, or condone the practice of it, while in their heart of hearts they know it to be unscriptural and ineffectual. An evangelical vicar of my acquaintance, sitting on a panel with other Christian leaders, was asked whether infant baptism really did anything for you. He replied that he himself had been 'christened, confirmed and vaccinated, and the only thing that took was vaccination!' We laugh with the rest, but when the laughter has died down we are left asking ourselves, 'How can this man continue to administer something he doesn't really believe in?'

There is undoubtedly truth in the covenant theology that lies behind infant baptism. One can see that the offspring of believing parents are not in the same category as those of unbelievers, if those parents are exercising faith for their infants.[2] But to introduce baptism as the means of expressing that difference is surely a misapplication of the ordinance, and is without any clear New Testament precedent. This is not the place for a lengthy discussion of the theological implications of the two positions; but the bold assertion I made earlier, that the practice of infant baptism was harmful, needs substantiating. So let us examine it pragmatically rather than doctrinally.

Creating a False Hope

The vast majority of British men and women with any church connection at all are linked with churches who practise infant baptism. It cannot be denied that most of them are unregenerate, and their allegiance is nominal. If asked they will usually affirm that they consider themselves to be Christians. Their proof? They were christened as babies. What else could the Prayer Book service for baptism mean when it speaks of the sprinkled infant as being received into the church, welcomed into the Lord's family, a member of the body of Christ?

Evangelical ministers are usually careful to explain to parents and godparents what is, in their view, the real significance of the rite, but the candidate, squealing in his mother's arms, is hardly a ready recipient for this information. If later he gets confirmed, is he likely to be told in confirmation classes (except in an evangelical church) that his christening didn't save him, and that he needs to be born again? Taking christendom at large, who can tell how many hundreds of thousands are living in a false hope in virtue of their christening?

Baptism is a rite of initiation, and most churches view it as the doorway to membership of the visible church. This compels those who practise infant sprinkling to adopt a certain view of the composition of the local church. They cannot view congregations of 'the visible church' as true communities of the redeemed, but as mixtures in which mere religious professors mingle with the regenerate. This touches the very foundation of the Christian community, and is an issue of such gravity that we must consider it separately in a subsequent chapter.

Separating What God Has Joined

Infant baptism separates practically two concepts that the Bible consistently joins together—repentance and faith on the one hand, and water baptism on the other. It also puts them in the reverse order.

John the Baptist 'preached repentance and baptism to all the people of Israel'.[3]

Jesus himself said, 'Whoever believes and is baptised will be saved.'[4]

Peter preached, 'Repent and be baptised...so that your sins may be forgiven.'[5]

Repentance and baptism belong together, and in that order. In the New Testament man first believed, and then sealed his faith in baptism. But this pattern is set aside by a practice which baptizes an infant in the hope that he will come to faith some future day. What God has joined it is not for us to put asunder.

Where Is the Joy of Obedience?

Our Lord made only two statements about water baptism, both of which were given in the context of commissioning his disciples, and both are of the greatest importance in relation to what we are discussing here. He said, 'Make disciples...baptising them....'[6] That puts the onus on the disciple-maker. He also said, 'Whoever believes and is baptised will be saved.'[4] That puts the onus on the convert, or the one being discipled. Notice how Ananias fulfilled his responsibility when he told the newly converted Saul of Tarsus, 'Get up, be baptised.'[7] But Saul had his part to play. He obeyed. Infant baptism, however, pre-empts this command of Christ to the convert. When a man is born again and wants to obey the Lord's command in baptism he is informed that he is already baptized. He was 'done' when he could have no say or active part in the proceedings. Infant baptism has robbed him of what is surely the greatest joy of baptism, obedience to one of Christ's commands.

Did Anything Happen?

Paedobaptists are not agreed as to what does or does not take place when an infant is christened. Some believe that the babe does become a child of God, as the Prayer Book implies. They subscribe to the doctrine of baptismal regeneration. Most evangelicals do not take that view, but believe that the child is not regenerate until he personally responds to Christ. They believe that God honours the faith of believing parents and godparents to that end. In favour of the baptismal regeneration position, it does at least invest the ordinance with some experiental significance for the candidate, which the other view does not.

The New Testament presents baptism as a confession of Christ. It is intended to signify for the convert, as we learn from the baptism of Saul of Tarsus, the washing away of his sins. It is to be an act of identification with Christ in his death and resurrection. How can an infant confess the Christ on whom he has not yet believed? How can there be a symbolic washing away of sins that have not yet been committed? And how can the rite signify a union with Christ that is still future?

An ordinance is neither solely symbolic nor automatically effectual or experiental. The genius of it is that the outward act is intended to trigger off faith for the spiritual fulfilment of what is being symbolized. In the case of baptism, when the new believer is plunged beneath the water, and then lifted up out of the water by a power outside himself, the outward act is to quicken faith within him for a spiritual fulfilment of what is being represented. He is saying to himself, 'Yes, praise God, *I have* died with Christ as far as my old life is concerned; *I have* been raised with him; and from now on *I am* walking with him in newness of life.' This vital experiental aspect is totally lost in infant baptism. In later years he will never recall the occasion. And even if he could, the sprinkling of a few drops of water on his head, and the making of the sign of the cross, would not convey to him what is graphically portrayed by the act of immersion.

A Missing Note in the Commission

As already pointed out, Jesus laid an onus on the disciple-maker to baptize those he discipled, as well as teaching them to observe all the things that he had commanded. We have already seen how Peter at Pentecost obeyed literally his Lord's command. Today, however, there seems to be a conspiracy of silence when it comes to any mention of water baptism in evangelistic preaching, except within churches that believe strongly in believers' baptism. That this should be the case with evangelists that come from a paedobaptist tradition is understandable, but it seems to be true of all interdenominational evangelists, even those who have themselves been immersed as believers, and know that this is the scriptural way.

There are those who will argue that this is right and proper. 'We don't want to be provocative or controversial, or offend those whose traditions are different from our own.' We shall see presently that Jesus was often provocatively controversial. He was also emphatic that we must not allow the traditions of men to make God's word of no effect. There is no justification for winking our eye at one of the items in the 'job description' that Christ gave us, while we obey the rest. If the basis on which we are conducting our evangelism requires us to compromise our message, we had better change the basis. Here is another situation where New Testament radicalism is needed in a situation of confusion and mixture.

Out of the Movement of the Spirit

It is an interesting and significant fact that many who in

these days have received the baptism in the Holy Spirit have also come to see, without any outside influence, the importance of being baptized by immersion. Down in the south-west where I used to live we experienced a stirring of the Spirit before the outbreak of the charismatic movement. Ron, a Cornish Methodist, was one whom the Lord touched. It was my privilege, with another brother, to minister to him. We made no mention of water baptism. Soon afterwards he wrote to tell me that he had been wakened in the night with the Scripture reference, 'Matthew 3:15', going over and over in his mind. Intrigued to know what it was, he turned on the bedside light and looked it up. He read the words of Jesus, asking the reluctant John the Baptist to immerse him. 'Let it be so now; it is proper for us to do this to fulfil all righteousness.' Ron had no doubt what God was saying, and his letter went on to recount how he had obeyed God, and how it proved to be even more of a joy-filled experience than his baptism in the Spirit.

If God is saying to you, 'Go and do likewise,' may I say two things. First, do not procrastinate. Some who have come to clear conviction on the issue have waited for 'a convenient season', and their delay has cost them their convictions. In the words of Ananias to Saul, 'And now what are you waiting for? Get up, be baptised.'[7] Second, if you belong to a church where infant baptism is practised, do not slip away for an 'under-the-counter' baptism in some other church. Honour the one who is over you in the Lord. Go and open your heart to your vicar or minister. Don't try to put him right over baptism. He won't appreciate that! Simply share the convictions you have reached and ask him to immerse you. If he is not willing to do that, ask him to release you to be baptized elsewhere. But be radical and see the thing through.

7

WITH WIND AND FIRE

We have seen that Peter's Pentecost sermon, in terms of Christian initiation, blazed a trail for succeeding generations of believers to follow, and involved the three-fold experience of repentance, water baptism and the reception of the Holy Spirit. In the fourth century after Christ, when state persecution gave way to state patronization, the church became more and more institutionalized, and the whole question of Christian initiation became blurred and confused. There was no longer a 'strait gate' at the entrance to the kingdom, and the world came pouring in. For the ship to be in the sea is right, but when the sea gets into the ship things are going perilously wrong. The invasion of the church by the world was a calamity from which christendom has never recovered, and for many centuries the professing church was largely in the dark concerning these radical terms of entry.

With the reformation came a rediscovery of justification by faith. God used the reformers to disentangle this vital truth from a doctrine of salvation by works that had obscured it. About the time this new light began to beam forth in Europe, companies of Christians practising the baptism of believers by immersion appeared in Germany and elsewhere. They were dubbed by their critics *Ana-*

baptists, people who got themselves *baptized again.* They stoutly denied what was implied in the nickname, for the very basis of their stand was that their infant christening had not fulfilled the conditions of New Testament baptism. For this they were outlawed and fiercely persecuted by the 'official church'. But the restoration of another foundation element of New Testament experience was under way.

Seasons of spiritual revival when God powerfully visited his people marked the centuries that followed. These brought the work of the Holy Spirit to the fore, and were often characterized by numbers of believers being 'filled', and by manifestations of the Spirit that people had assumed were confined to New Testament times. It was as though God would say, 'Look! I am still in the business, and what I did in the early church I can do today.' It is incredible that the modern view that equates the baptism in the Spirit with regeneration, and that implies 'we had it all at conversion', could have gained such widespread credence in the light of such overwhelming evidence to the contrary. When we find that our neat and tidy doctrine is being contradicted by what the Holy Spirit has done or is doing, it is time to take a second look at our doctrine. There is always the possibility we could have got it wrong.

Not till the dawn of the twentieth century was there a significant and permanent breakthrough concerning the baptism and gifts of the Holy Spirit. This came through the Pentecostal movement. Vilified and outlawed by the historic churches as the Anabaptists had been before them, the Pentecostals were compelled to form their own churches. For half a century the Pentecostal stream grew rapidly, especially through their overseas outreach, but made little or no impact on the non-Pentecostal stream. Then in the mid-sixties came God's second thrust. The charismatic movement broke out inside the historic churches and spread with little or no influence from classic Pentecostalism. Within fifteen years it had touched every major denomination of christendom and reached to the far corners of the earth.

Only One Baptism

It is important to see that baptism always speaks of *initiation,* and that is true of Spirit baptism as well as baptism in water. The two extremes we need to avoid in relation to the baptism in the Spirit are either mistakenly to identify it with the new birth, or to imply that those who have received it have 'arrived', as though it was a graduation certificate or a badge of proficiency. It was always new believers who received the Spirit. They do today wherever they are so taught, as they were in New Testament times.

When Paul talks about 'one baptism'[1] he is embracing both Spirit and water baptism. Together they comprise *the one baptism into Christ.* This is not a theological quibble, but a vital truth that cuts away much of the controversy and confusion that clusters around this theme. Israel's baptism into Moses is Paul's perfect picture of our baptism into Christ. 'Our forefathers were all under the cloud and ...they all passed through the sea. They were all *baptised into Moses in the cloud and in the sea.'*[2] This baptism did not take place *before* they were redeemed, nor *during* their wilderness wanderings, nor when they were about to enter Canaan. It took place at the time of their redemption, at the beginning of their pilgrimage. This was their *initiation* as God's people. They were said to be baptized into Moses as their deliverer, just as we are baptized into Christ. One baptism. But it was 'in the cloud and in the sea', prefiguring Spirit baptism and water baptism.

As we trace through the Acts record we find these two aspects of the one baptism are always linked. We have seen it was so in Peter's Pentecost sermon. But it was equally true on all the other occasions that the giving of the Spirit was recorded. At Samaria, Damascus, Caesarea and

Ephesus,[3] we find that Spirit baptism and water baptism go hand in hand. God views them as one, and when we do the same much of our misunderstanding disappears.

You can no more equate Spirit baptism with the act of regeneration than you can identify water baptism with the act of regeneration. The two baptisms are one. If it is possible for a regenerate person to be unbaptized in water it is just as possible for that same person to be unbaptized in the Spirit. The two baptisms are one. If it is inconceivable that God would ever baptize in the Spirit an unregenerate infant, it is surely improper that we should baptize that unregenerate infant in water. The two are one. What God has joined together let not man put asunder.

Just As It Should Be

Many charismatic leaders nowadays seem to favour dropping the expression *baptism in the spirit* for the less controversial *release of the Spirit*. This seems to indicate a trend to tone down the radical elements of the experience, to make it more 'respectable' and thus more acceptable to those who 'don't see it the way we do'. The idea of being immersed, enveloped, drenched in the Spirit sounds a bit sudden, extreme and overwhelming. It's not what some people are looking for or wanting. They would like the blessing of the Spirit provided it's reasonably quiet and orderly.

Observe how someone's blessing in the Spirit was described at a charismatic conference. 'He received the Spirit so quietly, without any emotion, and was released into a lovely prayer language, so beautiful and personal, *just as it should be.*' God meets with us all in different ways, and we must be thankful for every genuine experience of the Spirit. But notice the words I have italicized. The narrator is implying that a quiet, undemonstrative, unemotional experience, all very beautiful and personal, is the norm. Perhaps it has become the norm in what are nowadays called 'renewal circles', but what should be our criterion?

Back to the Beginning

God is not interested in accommodating his working to our background, our culture, our temperament, or our ideas of decorum and respectability. This was perfectly reflected in the life-style of the Son of God. He seldom observed protocol or allowed himself to be ruled by what was 'the done thing'. In fact he seemed at times to make a point of doing the very opposite. If therefore we wish to make a reappraisal of Spirit baptism, if we want to discover God's thoughts and feelings, once again it is no good referring back to church history, ecclesiastical tradition or evangelical opinion. We must trace the stream back to its source. We must look at God's original promise and how it was fulfilled.

Peter was God's chosen instrument to open the door of faith to the Gentiles. He would never forget the Gentile outpouring in the house of Cornelius. That visitation of the Spirit had unceremoniously brought his fine evangelistic sermon to an abrupt end. There were such spiritual fireworks as the Holy Spirit literally 'fell on all who heard the word'[4] that Peter could only recall his own glorious and never-to-be-forgotten baptism on the day of Pentecost, while the Jews accompanying him looked on in wide-eyed astonishment.

Later when Peter was asked by some of his colleagues in Jerusalem to account for his unorthodox behaviour in fraternizing with the Gentiles, he climaxed his explanation with these significant words: 'The Holy Spirit fell on them *just as on us at the beginning.*'[5] That was enough to convince the most sceptical that it was God, not Peter, who had initiated the whole affair. Where confusion or controversy surrounds a doctrine, or where we suspect that it has been adjusted, modified or watered down, it is good to go back and see how it was '*at the beginning*'.

With Wind and Fire

The first clear promise of the Spirit in the New Testament came from the lips of John the Baptist. It was a vital element in his testimony to the coming Messiah and is therefore recorded in each of the four gospels. He made it clear that his was only a water baptism, and that that of the Messiah would be 'with holy spirit and fire'. Using the other meaning of 'spirit'[6] we could translate the phrase, 'with holy wind and fire'. John was using a descriptive expression to help his hearers understand what this baptism would be like. It would involve the twin elements of wind and fire, and this is precisely what happened at Pentecost. The wind that bore down upon them symbolized God's power, and the fire that sat upon each of them spoke of his purity. The wind was coming to make them powerful, the fire to make them pure.

Look at this man Peter before Pentecost. Though he had confessed Jesus to be the Christ and had left all to follow him, we see a man who was still very insecure, involved in arguments with the other disciples as to who should be the greatest, jockeying for position, boasting that if all the others forsook Jesus, he would go with him to prison and to death, but in the event denying him with oaths and curses at the jibe of a servant girl. Then see him after Pentecost. What liberation of the whole personality has come to this man. Whether he is standing to preach before the assembled multitudes or standing for his life before the Jewish council, he is marked by the same incredible boldness, authority and faith. We have no difficulty in believing that the promise of John has been fulfilled in his case—he has been immersed in wind and fire.

It seems that in the move of the Spirit today we have lost sight of this basic characteristic of the baptism. Thank God for 'a lovely prayer language'. Speaking in tongues may be the normal manifestation of the Spirit coming upon a believer, but it is not the heart of the experience, and to make it such will result in serious loss. Tongues can never be enough if the wind and the fire are absent. In his farewell discourse before he ascended from Mount Olivet Jesus renewed to the disciples the promise of the Father. He could have said, 'You shall receive tongues when the Holy Spirit comes on you,' and that would have been quite true. But he said, 'You shall receive power.' Power was what they had been promised; power was what they believed for; and power was what they got. Only a church baptized in wind and fire will ever take the kingdom.

Noise and Emotion

I fully understand those who like it 'quietly, without any emotion'. When I first came in contact with the move of the Spirit in the fifties I brought with me a solid Anglo-Saxon temperament, a sensitive disposition and, for good measure, a conservative evangelical background! Any real display of noise or emotion I found embarrassing. If anybody had suggested that we start a Noise Abatement Society I would have volunteered to be a foundation member. I had been in meetings where the noise had been worked up, and where the enthusiasm was humanly ignited, like 'the strange fire' that Nadab and Abihu tried to offer to the Lord. But God had to teach me that my temperamental reserve and traditional conservatism was no more spiritual and no less carnal than noise that was 'out of the Spirit'. To allow my self-consciousness to rule my behaviour when God wanted to hear me clap or shout or 'make a joyful noise' was equally unacceptable to him.

What was it like 'at the beginning'? Was Pentecost

quiet and unemotional? The tongues speaking was so
noisy that it drew a vast crowd from right across the city.
Some came to listen, others to mock, but Peter still had
3,000 in the enquiry room at the end of his sermon.
Imagine that an onlooker grabs one of the apostles, and
the conversation goes like this:

'These people of yours are drunk with wine.'

'No, just filled with the Spirit.'

'They must be possessed.'

'Yes, God-possessed.'

'They have lost control of themselves.'

'The Spirit has taken over.'

'They are out of their minds.'

'They are lost in God.'

'But is God the author of all this noise?'

'Yes, he started it off. Didn't you hear that rushing
mighty wind? It came right in the middle of our lovely
prayer time.'

So Beautiful and Personal

We must not fall into the trap of over-personalizing spiritual experience, as evangelicalism has tended to do. 'A
personal faith in a personal Saviour' and 'a personal
baptism in the Spirit' present only one side of the truth.
Commitment to Christ is commitment to 'a body', and
baptism in the Spirit is baptism into 'a body'. There was
no individualism at Pentecost. The personal experience of
being 'filled' was quickly lost in an overwhelming sense of
oneness that coined a brand new word in our biblical
vocabulary—koinōnia, fellowship, the shared life. The
dynamic of the early church was not in Spirit-filled
individualism but in Spirit-filled corporeity. Even Peter's
great Pentecost sermon was not a solo performance, for
he 'stood up with the Eleven'.

When Paul states that 'we were all baptised in one Spirit

into one body'[7] he is not talking about regeneration. His theme in 1 Corinthians 12 is spiritual gifts and, judging by the list in verses 8–10, gifts of a 'charismatic' variety. And what brings God's people into the experience of such gifts? Not conversion as we all know, but a pentecostal baptism in the Spirit. To equate this baptism into the body with regeneration is not only out of keeping with the immediate context, but out of keeping with the other six references to Spirit baptism in the New Testament.

'Are you then suggesting,' someone will ask, 'that believers without this spirit baptism are not in the body of Christ?' No indeed. We must understand what being 'baptized into...' means in Scripture. John preached a baptism 'into repentance',[8] to translate his words literally. This did not mean people got baptized to bring them into a state of repentance, but when they had repented John baptized them into that repentance. Remember how he refused to baptize the Pharisees until they brought forth the fruit of repentance. Similarly with Christian baptism, only when a man is 'in Christ' do we have authority to baptize him into Christ. Water baptism never yet put a man in Christ. It is no different with Spirit baptism. Only those who are in the body of Christ by new birth are candidates for a baptism in the Spirit into that body.

We have already emphasized that water baptism is not merely symbolic but experiential. It is to quicken faith so that being 'in Christ' (i.e. united with him in his death, burial and resurrection) becomes a practical reality. Baptism in the Spirit is to make our position in the body of Christ truly functional in the power of the Spirit. To summarize, *baptism (whether water or Spirit) is to make truly experiential what is already positional*.

The unique feature of Pentecost was not 120 believers filled with the Spirit, but those Spirit-filled believers being fused into a functioning body, whose mighty corporate ministry was to turn the world upside down in the years that followed. The world had seen Spirit-filled persons before, but never a Spirit-filled body. Paul was always thinking corporately, and to him was given this revelation of what we might call the community dimension of the baptism in the Spirit. His illustration of Israel's baptism into Moses referred to a corporate experience.

The convert needs to be taught that the baptism in the Spirit is not primarily to make him a great preacher, pastor, evangelist or whatever, but to equip him to fit into his place in the body of Christ and function to his maximum efficiency. Individualism must be slain at the cross if that glorious corporate 'man' of Ephesians 4 is to stride the earth in the full plenitude of his manhood.

Needed—a Rich Outpouring

'Did you receive the Holy Spirit when you believed?'[9] was Paul's question to those first disciples in Ephesus. 'Did you receive the Spirit by observing the law, or by believing what you heard?'[10] was the question he posed to the Galatian churches. Both questions clearly imply that the reception of the Spirit was a clearly identifiable experience Always in his letters to the young churches he assumes that the Spirit has been received, just as he also assumes that they have all been baptized in water. If we had opportunity to ask Paul himself how he had received the Spirit his testimony would be as clear cut as that of Peter. He would take us back, not to his conversion on the Damascus road, but to the street called Straight, still to be seen in the old city of Damascus, and to the house of one called Judas, where an unknown disciple called Ananias laid hands on him so that he might receive his sight and be filled with the Spirit.[11]

Years later writing to Titus, his son in the faith, he spoke of the Holy Spirit's being 'poured out upon us richly'.[12] His use of that word 'richly' to describe his experience suggests firstly that it was no driblet that came upon him, it was an abundant, copious, generous outpouring. Then it conveys the thought of enrichment. Through this outpouring he had received invaluable gifts and endowments of the Spirit that were to bring permanent *enrichment* to his ministry, and through him to the body of Christ. But notice that Paul is not in fact personalizing. He doesn't say 'which he poured out upon me' but 'which he poured out upon *us*'. He is referring to himself, but he is also including Titus. He is actually making a general statement. He is saying, 'We have both had an abundant, copious, generous, glorious, enriching experience of the Spirit's outpouring' and implying that this was the New Testament norm. How many of us, even in charismatic circles, can honestly add our 'Amen'?

Don't Settle for Less

Have we been content with something less than the full consignment? Have we been satisfied with only a portion of our inheritance? Then we need to come to God, Elisha-like, for a double portion of the Spirit, and like that man of God, hold on till we get it. Let us encourage our brothers and sisters to do the same.

If we are radical Christians we shall never allow the fear that others may think us extreme to tone down what we believe about this radical experience. If we do we shall find that the cutting edge has gone, and not just for us, but for all those we want to influence. How we *view* the baptism in the Spirit will determine how we *speak* of it. How we *speak* of it will determine what people *believe for*. And what people *believe for* will determine what they *get*. And what they get should be nothing less than *a rich outpouring*, for that is the New Testament norm.

8

THE PRESCRIBED WAY

Religion has become formal and empty, simply going through the motions, but out of touch with spiritual reality. Religious leaders, by their rejection of God's word and God's standards, are stumbling, and making the people stumble too. Humanistic philosophy—man trusting in man for answers—prevails. No longer are there any absolutes. Good is called evil and evil good. Moral behaviour has consequently deteriorated alarmingly, as evidenced by bad language, lying, theft, dishonesty, mugging, murder, and every kind of violence. Heavy drinking and wild parties are all too common.

There is still plenty of money about, but people do not seem to see the extent of devaluation. Increased prosperity has brought increased idolatry—men have made materialism their god. They seem unaware of the growing signs of national decline. On the one hand there is bribery and corruption in high places, while in the lower echelons society tears itself apart, with one section of the community warring against another. No longer do the young show any respect for the aged or the honoured in society. They are flexing their political muscles and entering the arena of power and influence. Women, too, are joining the fight for liberty and equality, and grasping the reins of leadership. Spiritual decline is also seen in the increase of eastern occultism. More and more are turning to spiritist mediums for answers.

A picture of today's western world? We could be excused for thinking so, but in fact we are looking at the northern and southern kingdoms of Israel through the eyes of two of their prophets. This was how the prophecy of Hosea and the first eight chapters of Isaiah describe the spiritual and moral state of Israel more than seven centuries before Christ. The prophetic books are certainly 'tracts for the times'. This was a period of great fear and insecurity. Away to the east was the ascendant star of Assyria, making its bid for world dominion, much as the Soviet Union today. Why, asks the prophet, should men go to occult spirits of the dead for answers, when they have the living God? *'To the law and to the testimony!'* he cries. That's where we need to look for an authentic word. 'If they do not speak according to this word, they have no light of dawn.'[1]

The question we must each face in this chapter is, Does the Scripture have a 'now word' for my current situation? It may speak truly concerning my relationship with God, but what about my relationship with the world of the micro-chip? It may speak with clarity concerning my personal life, but what about my church life in a confused and divided christendom? Nearly two millennia have passed since the New Testament was penned. Can a first-century document really have twentieth-century relevance? 'Yes, of course,' orthodoxy will be quick to answer. But like those who are ready to cry, 'Lord, Lord,' the acid test is when it comes to translating lip service into the hard cash of obedience. It is a question of living 'according to scripture'[2] in *every* department of our lives. In this chapter let us test our attitude to the Bible. If it is right, then our response to what God may be pleased to reveal to us will always be radical.

Under Attack

In the garden Satan opened his attack, not with a categorical denial of what God had said—that was to come later—but with a subtle insinuation calculated to sow doubt: 'Did God really say...?'[3] His tactics have not changed. Certain publications coming off the Christian press are posing some very important questions as to what we can believe and what we should believe regarding the accuracy and reliability of Holy Scripture on the matters of which it treats. In asking whether we can believe in the historicity of Jonah and the whale, or whether the wise men from the east were fact or fiction, we are asking the wrong questions and failing to concern ourselves with the root issue. Though it may seem trite to say it, our attitude to the Bible will always be determined by our attitude to God. If our attitude to him is right, so will be our attitude to his word.

At the close of World War 2 I was serving with the British Army in the Mediterranean theatre. Training courses to help service personnel prepare for their jobs in civilian life were arranged. The only thing I could find that offered anything to someone who wanted to serve God was a course on philosophy and New Testament Greek for ordinands. Not quite what I would have ordered, but better than nothing.

The course was held in the university town of Perugia. There I met an enthusiastic army padre. His view of the Bible was very different from my own, and we crossed swords more than once. Some of the questions he raised I had no difficulty in answering, but others threw me off balance. I spent some days in Doubting Castle.

What brought me out was not finding answers to my intellectual difficulties, but allowing the Holy Spirit to bring me back to those things that I had experienced of the grace of God: the reality of being forgiven and accepted by God; Bible promises of God's provision that I had proved; war experiences of God's miraculous protection, as with the enemy shell that landed a couple of feet from my slit trench and would have blown me to smithereens had it exploded; and much else. God was real. God was there. He had spoken in his word, and I had proved the truth of it again and again. There are still many unanswered questions, but the thirty-five years that have passed since that experience in Perugia have only served to deepen my confidence in and love for this Book.

Restoration and the Fear of the Lord

Yes, our attitude to the Bible, even how we interpret it and respond to it, will always be determined by our relationship with God. Scripture and history both teach us that times of revival and of restoration are times of great hunger and reverence for God's word, because men are made overwhelmingly aware of God's presence. The attitude to the divine word is simply a reflection of the attitude to the divine Person. It is inconceivable that people could have a consuming hunger for God and at the same time be careless and indifferent to his word.

The prophets, and the restoration prophets in particular, displayed the fear of God to a high degree. Some of the greatest prayers of the Bible came from the lips of Ezra, Nehemiah and Daniel, men who were caught up in God's great restoration programme. We find them humbling themselves with prayer and fasting. They address 'the great and awesome God, who keeps his covenant of love with all who love him and obey his commands'.[4] They abject themselves before God as they confess the sins of the people who have despised God's holy law. 'I am too ashamed and disgraced to lift up my face to you, my God, because our sins are higher than our heads and our guilt has reached to the heavens,' prays Ezra.[5]

The same spirit that causes these men to tremble before the God of heaven causes them to tremble before his word. 'Daniel,' said the heavenly messenger who had come to give him understanding of the vision he had seen, 'you who are highly esteemed, consider carefully the words I am about to speak to you, and stand up, for I have now been sent to you.' Daniel records his response: 'And when he said this to me, I stood up trembling.'[6] With what awe and holy fear did these great saints receive the word of God. When Ezra discovered how the exiles had broken the law by intermarrying with foreigners he records, 'I tore my tunic and cloak, pulled hair from my head and beard and sat down appalled. Then *everyone who trembled at the words of the God of Israel* gathered around me.'[7] So the radical reaction of the man of God had a profound effect on the people.

Head or Heart?

One of the greatest snares we face in connection with the Bible is intellectualism. Having come into the kingdom by believing God's word in the heart, we then tend to revert to apprehending truth by our natural mental processes. Facts are stored in the brain, but truth is not assimilated into the spiritual bloodstream, because there is no vital operation of faith. The pastor of a large congregation in the USA once expressed to me his concern over the use of teaching cassettes. In his flock there had been a number of conversions from the professional classes. They were eager to learn and to grow, and with their trained minds they were using tapes to master spiritual themes just in the same way as they had become proficient in their own fields of learning. But spiritual knowledge does not spell spiritual edification. So often faith is the missing ingredient, and the sphere of operation is the head rather than the heart.

In speaking of fearing God and trembling at his word

we are talking about heart condition. This is the crux of the matter. God says, 'This is the one I esteem: he who is humble and contrite in spirit, and trembles at my word.'[8] Where there is a whole-hearted submission to the will of God there will always be an awe of God's word, a radical response of obedience to specific issues, and a reaction of deep concern when God shows us that we have fallen short. Where this heart condition is lacking there is an easy-going carefree attitude to truth, failure to be 'careful to obey' what he has commanded us (like King Jehu), and a readiness to excuse or justify when the Holy Spirit finds us out.

Father and Son

These two opposing attitudes are vividly demonstrated in the lives of two kings of Judah. During the reign of Josiah the Book of the Law had been discovered in the temple. It was read to the King by his secretary. Josiah's reaction was dramatic. He tore his robes and sent his officials immediately to enquire of the Lord concerning what had been read. He knew that God meant what he said and that his judgement was hanging over the nation because, in his own words, 'our fathers have not obeyed the words of this book; they have not acted in accordance with all that is written there concerning us.'[9] God's answer was that judgement would surely come, but that the axe would not fall in Josiah's reign because of his right reaction— 'because your heart was responsive and you humbled yourself before the Lord when you heard what I have spoken…and because you tore your robes and wept in my presence.' A time of revival followed.

It was in the reign of Jehoiakim, a son of Josiah, that the Babylon army invaded the land, and the prediction of judgement began to be fulfilled. Nevertheless there was still time to repent and for judgement to be averted.

Repeated warnings were being given to the King and the nation through the prophet Jeremiah. At God's instruction he dictated to Baruch his scribe all the words he had spoken since the reign of Josiah, and told him to read the scroll to the people assembled in the temple. As a result the scroll was eventually brought to King Jehoiakim. As each portion was read by the scribe the King cut it off with a knife and threw it into the brazier that was burning before him, until the whole scroll was consumed. He showed not the slightest concern over what he had heard. In fact his only reaction was to issue an order for the arrest of Jeremiah and Baruch.

What the father possessed that was totally lacking in the son was the fear of the Lord. Most of us fall somewhere between these two. We are not guilty of the cold indifference of Jehoiakim. But nor do we emulate the fervour for God's word that we see in Josiah. Perhaps we need to ask ourselves if ours is the non-radical response of the lukewarm.

The Prescribed Way

It is not enough that we apply all that has been said to our personal lives. God has much to say in Scripture concerning our corporate life. He has not left us without clear direction as to the appointments of his house, and how we are to function as part of it. Our church life is to be conformed to God's word. For some, this is where the shoe may pinch. A radical determination to know and do God's will is as important here as anywhere else.

At the heart of the Old Testament worship was the ark of the covenant that usually resided in the Holy of Holies. Its career after the Israelites had entered the land of Canaan had been rather a chequered one. Captured by the Philistines in battle, it had eventually been returned to Israel, but had never been restored to a central place in the life of the nation. At the outset of his reign David determined to alter this. He told the people, 'Let us bring the ark of our God back to us, for we did not enquire of it during the reign of Saul.'[10]

How often we read, David *enquired* of the Lord.'[11] That was his usual procedure before any undertaking. This time, however, David *conferred* with each of his officers'.[12] So instead of a prayer meeting he held a committee meeting. It came up with 'a good idea'. Committee meetings usually do. Carrying the ark with poles on the shoulders of the priests may have been all right during their desert wanderings, but their religious life had developed since those primitive days. Why be tied to the slow and laborious way it was done in the beginning? Why not imitate the Philistines and transport it on a new cart?[13] The motion was carried unanimously. Perhaps they closed the committee meeting with a prayer for God's blessing on their plan. If so, God didn't hear it. He has never committed himself to bless our plans. He prefers to bless what he himself has initiated.

We remember the tragic outcome of this venture. The oxen drawing the cart stumbled. Uzzah, one of the two men leading the cart, put out his hand to steady the ark. And God struck him dead. Why such a severe judgement? God wanted this incident to be a flashing red light for all time, warning God's people under the New Covenant, as well as under the Old, that it is foolish and dangerous when handling the things of God's house to alter what God has prescribed. If we have the fear of the Lord we shall not attempt it. Nor will we want to perpetuate changes that others have wrongly initiated.

It took a hurt, angry and frightened David three months to recover from this experience. But he came to terms with what God was saying. Before he attempted it again he summoned the priests and the Levites, and said to them, 'It was because you, the Levites, did not bring [the

ark] up the first time that the Lord our God broke out in
anger against us. *We did not enquire of him about how to
do it in the prescribed way.*'[14] Had they *enquired* instead of
conferred God would surely have reminded them of what
he had laid down. So in the end 'the Levites carried the
ark of God with the poles on their shoulders, as *Moses had
commanded in accordance with the word of the Lord*'.[15]

The Appointments of God's House

Since most of us are fairly particular concerning the
appointments in our own houses, it would be surprising to
find that God took a happy-go-lucky attitude towards his.
In fact God is exceedingly 'house proud'. When the first
sanctuary was to be constructed he left nothing to man's
whim or fancy, but gave Moses explicit instructions, down
to the last pin and socket, as to what he wanted. He even
took him on a conducted tour of a heavenly model and
told him, 'I want it just like that.'[16] It was the same with
Solomon's temple. David gave him the plans 'that the
Spirit had put in his mind'. It was all in writing by 'the
hand of the Lord'.[17] It was not even left to the wisdom of
Solomon.

If God was so meticulous under the Old Covenant, can
we imagine him being any less under the New? Like
Solomon, we too have it all in writing by the hand of the
Lord in the pages of the New Testament. But for us there
is a very important difference:

In the Old Testament God had a sanctuary for his
people; in the New God has his people for a sanctuary.

In the Old Testament we have a material house; in the
New we have a spiritual house.

In the Old Testament there was a divine 'pattern'; in
the New there are divine principles.

With the one there is a fixed form; with the other there
is a flexible body.

When men impose on the congregation a rigid and uniform structure, whether it is of the traditional and historic variety, or based on the mistaken assumption that there is an inflexible New Testament 'pattern' for church life, they are going back 'under law'. There is no evidence that the New Testament churches were like peas in a pod. That would have been contrary to the genius of the Spirit. God is a God of variety, and there are always varieties of style with differences of race and culture. But with all the diversity of form the same principles come shining through. The similarities are more important than the differences. It is not forms but principles that should concern us.

Man's Interference

Can you imagine the feelings of a couple who, having allowed some friends to make use of their home, return to find the furnishings have been drastically altered? The piano in the lounge has been moved to the other side of the room. Valuable oil paintings have been taken down and stored in the attic, and the lovely curtains in the dining room have been replaced by some others with a ghastly design. It is difficult to believe that anyone could have such audacity; but this is, in effect, what christendom has done with God's house over the centuries. Changes were effected so slowly that men were hardly aware that they were happening, or how far they had departed from New Testament church life. The periods of change were simultaneous with periods of spiritual decline.

Though God's ways for his church are always the best they are so designed that they will only function with divine power. With the decline of true godliness the Holy Spirit gradually withdrew, so men, instead of rectifying the evil and securing the return of the Spirit, looked round for human expedients, ways of keeping the wheels turning apart from the Spirit. That necessitated the introduction of much that God had never ordained. In this way some things were thrown out that should have been kept in, and some things were brought in that should have been kept out.

These tragic developments in church history were all clearly foreshadowed, if men could only have seen it, in the history of King Ahaz. He was a deeply religious man, but he struck a body blow at 'the prescribed way' of drawing near to God when he removed the altar of burnt offering (which typifies the cross) from its central position, and made it a bloodless vehicle for seeking God's guidance. In its place he introduced a heathen altar that had caught his fancy on a visit to Damascus.[18] This led to a whole range of changes and innovations. In the space of two incredible verses we read that 'King Ahaz took away...and removed.... He removed.... He took away ...and removed....'[19] This is what has happened in church history. Every removal spells loss, and every loss needs to be recovered, for nothing God planned for his house is superfluous.

The revivals under Hezekiah and Josiah saw the removal from the temple of every unclean thing. Anything in the Holy Place that God has not prescribed is unclean. Thank God we are living in a time of the restoration of God's house, and that not only means a time of recovery of so much that has been lost, but also a time when radical and often painful steps must be taken to remove all that man has introduced. The Christian who is radical, who trembles at God's word, will not allow tradition, sentiment, personal preference, or anything else to prevent him from conforming to what he knows is God's prescribed way.

9

TESTING THE STRUCTURE

A friend of mine bought a house only to discover after occupying it for a while that there was dry rot in the structure. He had been informed when he bought it that there had been this kind of trouble in the past, but had been assured by the vendor that it had been completely eradicated. Clearly the treatment had not been sufficiently radical, and now he was having to face at great cost and inconvenience the stripping of plaster and ripping out of timbers as workmen sought to get at the source of the trouble. Unfortunately there was no alternative. We all know that a building with dry rot has no future.

We have been facing up to our attitude to the word of God, and in particular to that word as it declares God's mind concerning his house. We have seen how God gave instruction under the Old Covenant concerning the construction, appointments and functioning of his sanctuary. I spoke of the serious and widespread departure of the churches of christendom from God's 'prescribed way', but it was all in general terms. We must now take this a stage further and see how vital it is that our church structures conform to the New Testament.

Whitewashing a Flimsy Wall

In the case of my friend's house, he and his family suffered because 'the professionals' were not thorough. Affected parts were plastered over only to compound the problem by allowing the disease to spread. This has happened again and again in the history of the church, and I fear it is happening now in the charismatic renewal. God's family suffers because 'the professionals', the spiritual builders, the men in leadership who are meant to know, have shrunk from applying the radical treatment that decaying church structures require, and have contented themselves with superficial treatment. The interior may look spick and span as a result of 'operation renewal' but this will not save the house in the coming storm if the structures are faulty and flimsy.

God spoke stern words to prophets in Ezekiel's day who fostered in the nation an optimism and a security that was wholly unjustified.

> Because they lead my people astray saying, 'Peace', when there is no peace, and because, when a flimsy wall is built, they cover it with whitewash, therefore tell those who cover it with whitewash that it is going to fall. Rain will come in torrents, and I will send hailstones hurtling down, and violent winds will burst forth . . . I will tear down the wall you have covered with whitewash and will level it to the ground so that its foundation will be laid bare.[1]

Surely no one can doubt the warnings in Scripture of the end-time shaking, for it is already upon us. Everything that can be shaken will be shaken. Men will then see what is the quality of our church foundations and structures, for 'the day will declare it'.

Beware the Patching Operation

In the time of our Lord when men, groaning under the

slavery of Judaism, were sensing that a new era was dawning, Jesus warned them in the clearest terms that the new thing that he was inaugurating could not be limited by the old, nor could it be used to patch it. He said, according to Matthew, 'No-one sews a patch of unshrunk cloth on an old garment, for the patch will pull away from the garment, making the tear worse.'[2] Though the immediate effect is good, in the long term the tear ends up not mended but extended.

A church is not fully renewed if the structures are left untouched. To have within a traditional church a live group composed of those who have received the Spirit and are beginning to move in spiritual gifts; to introduce a freer and livelier spirit into the worship with renewal songs; to permit the clapping and lifting up of hands and even the dance; to split the week-night meeting into home groups for purposes of discipling; to replace 'a one-man leadership' with a team of elders—all these measures, good though they are, will only prove to be a patching operation. Individuals will undoubtedly be blessed. There will be an initial quickening of the church. But if it ends there, the long-term results will be detrimental. There will be a quiet struggle going on between the new measures and the old structures, and you may be sure the old structures will win in the end.

Luke's account of Jesus' words enlightens us further: 'No-one *tears a patch from a new garment* and sews it on an old one. If he does, *he will have torn the new garment,* and the patch from the new will not match the old.'[3] The focus shifts from the tattered garment to the piece of unshrunk cloth. Luke tells us where it came from. It was not bought from a remnant shop, or an odd piece the tailor had left over, it was *torn from a new garment.* Here is the second argument against the patching operation: it spoils the new thing. When God creates something new it is complete and whole in itself, like a garment. God does not intend men to cut it up for patching, choosing what they want and rejecting the rest. But the alternative, as those Jewish disciples of Christ were soon to find out, is pretty radical. It is to cast off the tattered garment and replace it with the new. The first half of the book of Acts records the struggle of the Jewish church in going through with this.

The final argument is that 'the new will not match the old'. The word 'match'[4] is significant. It is used of stones in a building that *fit together* at their joints; of notes that *harmonize* to make music; and here, of materials that *match* in colour or texture. The new patch will never blend in with the old garment, so as to become part of it. It will always look incongruous. In the early days of the charismatic movement I expressed to one of its foremost leaders my doubts as to whether all that God was bestowing by his Spirit could ever be truly *integrated* into the life of historic churches, unless those churches were prepared for radical reform. At that time he was full of optimism on this issue. Sadly, the intervening years have proved that his optimism was ill-founded, and the words of Jesus have, as always, been vindicated. We are up against a principle of incompatibility in the spiritual realm.

Now we must stop generalizing and be specific. Since the church is composed of living stones, when we talk about New Testament structure we are not talking about organization but people. In bringing the structure of the local congregation to the touchstone of Scripture, and in no area is this more important, we are enquiring as to what sort of people should constitute that congregation. I believe that we shall come to see that in the biblical view the local body has an *all-believing* membership, that all believers are *priests,* and that all have a *ministry*. This is no company of pew-warmers or hangers-on, but *committed people* who have been knitted and joined together.

The Myth of the Mingled Church

Emperor Constantine, as we have already seen, opened the door of the church to the world. The *Encyclopaedia Britannica* in its entry 'The Church' has this significant statement:

> The fact that many Christians hold nominal beliefs and do not act like the followers of Christ has been noted since the 4th Century when the church ceased to be persecuted. To account for this, St Augustine proposed that the real church is an invisible entity known only to God. [5]

On the other side Augustine also taught that the 'visible church' on earth was a mixture, consisting not only of true believers, members of the 'invisible church', but of those who were mere professors, hypocrites and the like. This he termed 'the mingled church'.

In the early days of the reformation Luther saw that this was an accommodation, and that it fell far short of the ideal. In 1526 he wrote:

> The right kind of evangelical order cannot be exhibited among all sorts of people. But those who are seriously determined to be Christians and confess the gospel with hand and mouth, must enrol themselves by name and meet apart, in one house, for prayer, for reading, to baptise, to take the sacrament, and exercise other Christian works. With such order it would be possible for those who did not behave in a Christian manner to be known, reproved, restored or excluded, according to the rule of Christ. . . . But I cannot yet order and establish such an assembly, for I have not yet the right people for it.

One church historian, quoting the above, has this comment to make:

> Yet Luther knew that 'the right people' were there; people whom he described as 'true, pious, holy children of God'. After much hesitation he came at last to oppose any attempt to put into practice what he had so excellently portrayed. [6]

The Real Reason

The practice of infant baptism and the concept of 'a mingled church' go hand in hand. The early church fathers embraced these doctrines not because they discovered them in Scripture, but because they were expedients to meet a situation that had developed. Put a New Testament into the hands of a group of converts without any previous Christian knowledge, and ask them to search out what it teaches about baptism. How many would come up with a doctrine of infant baptism? Similarly, if they went through the church epistles to find out how Paul viewed the congregations he was addressing, how many would endorse the opinion of Calvin, who saw the membership of the visible church as necessarily including 'a very large mixture of hypocrites, who have nothing of Christ but the name and outward appearance'.[7]

If baptism means initiation, if it is 'the rite of entry into the church', an infant necessarily becomes a member on being christened. This guarantees that the local church will always contain unregenerate members. And when the infant becomes an adult, still without making any personal response to Christ, there is no de-baptizing procedure, or removing of that name from the roll of membership. Accept the practice of infant baptism as right and a mixed congregation is the inevitable result. Generally speaking a baptized member of a denomination today has a right of membership in the local church of that denomination, to exercise his power to vote on issues brought before the church, and no minister has authority to preclude him even though he knows him to be unregenerate.

God's way is that the children of believing parents are 'sanctified' by the faith of those parents, until they reach the age of accountability. However, there must be a personal response when they are able to understand the gospel if they are to become a part of the local congregation.

Clarifying the Issues

Those who defend this concept of 'the mingled church' decry what has recently been described as 'the constant tendency to cream off from the visible church a spiritual elite to form a pure fellowship'.[8] If by 'a spiritual elite' and 'a pure fellowship' is meant churches, like the New Testament ones, composed only of those who are born again, then I plead guilty, not to a tendency, but to a conviction. But so often there is the implication that anyone who takes this view is setting up an impossible standard, and that those who make such claims for their churches are lacking in both humility and reality. Let us be clear: we are arguing that no one has right of membership in the church apart from the new birth. We are not demanding a high standard of spirituality or maturity in order to belong.

Calvin argued that Paul acknowledged Corinth as 'a church of Christ and a society of saints' even though 'almost the whole body had become tainted' with numerous blemishes which he catalogued at length. 'If there the church still remains,' he maintained, 'who will presume to deny the title of church to those to whom a tenth part of these crimes cannot be imputed?'[9]

In the first place Paul didn't merely call the Corinthians 'a church'. He said they were 'God's building' and 'God's temple'[10] and 'the body of Christ'.[11] That doesn't seem to imply that he viewed them as a mixture of saved and lost. More significantly, he reminded them of their regeneration when, despite their many failings, he wrote, 'But you were washed, you were sanctified, you were justified in the name of the Lord Jesus Christ and by the Spirit of our God.'[12] If Paul ever addressed those words to a mixed church he was guilty of grave pastoral irresponsibility. No, they were true believers, despite their carnality. Paul was seeking to restore them to spirituality.

The Church and the Kingdom

The major argument for a church of mixture is based on Jesus' parable of the tares of the field. When the servants wanted to pull up the tares the owner refused, lest in doing so they root up the wheat with them. The time of separation would be at the harvest. Fortunately we have Jesus' own interpretation of this parable. He never said 'the field is *the church*'; but he did say 'the field is *the world*'.[13] In the sphere of world-wide profession, which is the meaning of 'kingdom' in these parables, we cannot always discern with infallibility who are, and who are not 'the wheat'. But Scripture never says, 'The Lord *alone* knows those who are his.' It simply states, 'The Lord knows those who are his,'[14] and as a general rule, we too should be able to distinguish those who are *for* Christ from those who are *against* him. At least we should be able to do so within the closely-knit community of God's people. Ought a man to be the shepherd of a flock if he cannot discern between sheep and goats?

All this is not to suggest that we equate the church membership roll with 'the Lamb's book of life'. We occasionally make mistakes. They made them in the early church. There were those who 'secretly slipped in',[15] those who 'went out' because 'they did not really belong'[16] and those who did not dare join because they knew that they had to be real.[17] But all that only proves what was the rule concerning the composition of New Testament churches.

The Discipline Issue

Let us go back to the beginning, as we did regarding the baptism in the Spirit, and see what the words of the Founder and Head of the church have to teach us on this issue. He introduced the concept of the church in its universal and its local aspect in two germinal statements, one in Matthew 16 and the other in Matthew 18. The local church concept is introduced in the context of your brother having sinned against you. To get him alone and show him his fault is the first step. If he will not listen, you take one or two other brothers along and confront him again. If he won't listen to them either, you are to tell it to the church. And if even that does not bring him to heel, the final act is a pronouncement of discipline by the whole congregation.

All this is to teach us what store Christ put on the maintaining of fellowship, and the lengths to which we must go to restore it. But that presupposes a relationship among the members that could not exist if some were unregenerate. Further, would it not be wholly inappropriate, not to mention unworkable, to involve unbelievers in the pronouncement of discipline on a believer? Should they not be looking to their own spiritual state? Paul thought it was scandalous that believers in the Corinthian church were taking their disputes before unbelievers in the law courts. Luther, as we have shown, saw so clearly in the beginning that only truly converted people can be 'reproved, restored or excluded, according to the rule of Christ'. What a tragedy he did not implement it. Pity help the shepherd who tries to discipline the goats.

This question of the structure of the local church is not a minor issue. We need look no further for reasons why christendom is such a spiritual hotch-potch. Is it not also the reason why men who are unregenerate and unspiritual, men who even deny the basics of the faith, are able to attain to high ecclesiastical office simply on the basis of scholarship and ability? They would never even have qualified for church membership in New Testament times.

In our quest for the structure of the local church as taught and exemplified in the New Testament, we find that not only is every member a believer, but every believer is a priest.

The Great Change

It is generally agreed that the New Testament church was modelled on the synagogue and not on the temple.[18] The development of synagogue worship after Israel's return from captivity was one of God's ways of preparing the church-to-be for the tremendous leap out of Judaism into Christianity, for 'the institution of synagogues was flexible enough to allow free scope for wide divergencies of creed and practice'.[19] The temple with its fixed forms and ceremonies was far less vulnerable to the gospel than was the synagogue. It is significant that the first threat to the life of the new churches came from Judaizers, propounding a mixture of law and grace. Galatians and Hebrews are particularly addressed to this deviation from the gospel. The institutionalizing of the church which developed after the New Testament era was nothing more than Judaism breaking forth in another guise.

When we leave the picture of the churches as Scripture presents them, and plunge into the history of the succeeding centuries, we are immediately aware that a profound change has taken place. How come the development of a priestly caste wearing special vestments and adopting special titles? How is it that churches are now worshipping in 'consecrated buildings', with fixed forms of service, with rites and ceremonies, and numerous other ecclesiastical innovations? It is certain that none of this came from the New Testament. Little of it was inspired by the synagogue. The source of inspiration was the temple worship of the Old Testament. Only here do we find a priestly caste, priestly vestments, priestly rites and ceremonies, and the use of sacred buildings.

The old legalism has dropped its front runner of New Testament times, circumcision. That was useful among the Jews but not among the Gentiles. But the same principle of law is at work, robbing the churches of their God-given freedom. To put the New Testament church—which God had intended to be a dynamic, liberated community—into an Old Covenant strait-jacket was the master stroke of the devil.

We may wonder how such changes were ever allowed to come about. It happened slowly, in the context of spiritual decline, and when those who 'trembled at God's word' were few and far between. In due course a theory of 'development' was propounded. This argued that the church life and ministry that began to emerge in the time of the apostles was 'primitive', 'temporary', or 'embryonic', as we see it described in Scripture, and as the church grows up we must allow for changes and developments. This was the justification for wholesale departure from New Testament principles. But remember, it was not a forward movement into greater simplicity, flexibility and freedom, which is the genius of the New Testament church, but backwards into the rigidity of the Old Covenant system.

The Great Divide

Of all these developments none was more detrimental in the long term than the return to the priestly caste of the Old Testament. It brought a great divide between priests and people. It divided the flock of God into clergy and laity. It shackled the bulk of every congregation in ignorance, passivity and non-involvement. All priestly functions were now left to 'the professionals'. 'Weren't they paid to do the job?'

Nowhere in the New Testament is 'priest' used to describe a leader or officer in the church. The message of Hebrews is clear and plain. When our great High Priest 'had offered for all time one sacrifice for sins'[20] the Old Testament priesthood was wound up for ever, and every believer is now constituted a priest, entitled to offer up spiritual sacrifices in the house of God. It is not strictly accurate to say that there is no longer a sacrificing priesthood. It is rather that the type of sacrifice has changed. We no longer offer *sacrifices for sin*. If the Roman mass claims to be an offering up of the body and blood of Christ we reject that claim outright. It could only cast a grave reflection on the sufficiency of that one perfect sacrifice. But we do offer up praise, prayer and worship, and these are called 'spiritual sacrifices'.

The totally unscriptural distinction between clergy and laity is now openly acknowledged, even from within the establishment.[21] The doctrine of 'the priesthood of all believers' has long been a tenet of the faith, at least among evangelicals. More and more church leaders are involving the people in various aspects of ministry. Despite all this the divide between clergy and laity is still there, and still clogging the chariot wheels. The full potential of the body of Christ will never be fully released until this wretched distinction is wholly removed. This is not likely to happen so long as those who avow it to be wrong perpetuate it by retaining their clerical office, using their clerical title and wearing their clerical garb. A man may assert that 'the divide' is unbiblical, but no one is likely to take him seriously until he breaks free from an establishment that could not exist without it. It is certainly costly to be a radical.

A Different Concept of Ministry

Once the clergy/laity distinction is removed the concept of ministry changes. It ceases to be the proprietary right of the few and becomes the privilege of all. Obviously this does not imply that all qualify as leaders, or that all have the same ministry. Some are still called to particular service by the Head of the church. For this there is the scriptural practice of the laying on of hands to set apart, commission, and impart grace, performed by those spiritually qualified to do it. But this is a far cry from much that goes by the name of 'ordination'.

It is unfortunate that biblical words like 'minister' and 'ministry' have become shrouded by ecclesiastical concepts, and therefore signify to us something very different from the simple meanings attached to them in Scripture. People still think of 'the minister' exclusively in terms of a leader, whose different dress marks him out as specially trained and qualified to do what lesser mortals cannot. He alone can perform in the church, and what he performs is his 'ministry'. It might prove salutary to cut these terms right out of our vocabulary, and simply talk about 'the servant' and 'his service', which are the real meanings, and apply them to *all* the people, not just the leaders.

A Serving Body

God's heart must be grieved when he sees the gifts that he has liberally bestowed on his people finding no room for expression in the local church where they primarily belong. The consequence has been that gifted men and women have sought avenues of service outside the church, to its further impoverishment. This in turn has resulted in the proliferation of para-church organizations, most of which would not have been necessary if the church had been functioning properly. God has chosen the church for the work of his kingdom. Biblically structured and anointed with the Holy Spirit, it is the best, the most efficient instrument for the job in hand. The answer to the need of the hour is not in para-church substitutes, but in Spirit-filled restored churches. I say again, it is foolish to try to be wiser than God.

Just as in a human body every organ has a function, and that function provides a service to the whole of the body, so it is in the spiritual body. Every believing member, even the youngest and feeblest, has an essential service to render. 'Those parts of the body that seem to be weaker are indispensable, and the parts that we think are less honourable we treat with special honour.'[22] The factor that determines the nature of each man's service or contribution is the anointing and gift of the Spirit. Just as Scripture does not anticipate a church member being unconverted or unbaptized, neither does it anticipate him being ungifted. '*To each one* the manifestation of the Spirit is given for the common good.'[23] As Howard Snyder has put it, 'According to the New Testament, the church is a charismatic organism, not an institutional organization.'[24] We have seen how church history in a negative way confirmed this. As the Holy Spirit withdrew, institutionalism took over to try to keep the organization going.

Paul's vision and passion was for the church to come to corporate maturity, to be that new man of full stature in the earth by building itself up in love. But that is only possible '*when each part is working properly*'.[25] Such a concept of a functioning body allows for no passengers, no sleeping partners, no spare parts. It not only presupposes that each member possesses divine life, but that he is wholly committed to the body of which he is a part.

No Double Standard

They were not periphery people, 'half in–half out' Christians, those members of the early church. Their salvation involved a commitment to Christ, and the quality of that commitment was expressed by their involvement in the corporate life of the congregation. In the church to which I currently belong we do not receive every professed believer who applies for membership. Marriage is a mutual commitment, and so is joining a church. That is why, except in the case of new converts, a courting period is needed. Coming from a mixed or confused background, a believer must know what is required of him as a member, and what he in turn may expect from this local body and its leaders.

Christ taught that our commitment to him must be whole-hearted. It means denying oneself, taking up the cross and following him. But Scripture is equally clear that our attitude to Christ is reflected by our attitude to his people.[26] As is our attitude to the Head, so will be our attitude to his body. You cannot be whole-hearted towards Christ but only half-hearted towards his church. To belong should mean to be totally committed.

Without such an understanding by the sheep as to what it means to be part of the flock, proper shepherding will be ineffective. A shepherd must know who is truly in his flock, as distinct from the roving sheep who come to sample the pasture. If he is uncertain about whether a person is really committed to the flock and submitted to his shepherding care, how can he ever bring admonition and correction when that becomes necessary? Where commitment is vague, relationships will be loose, and that means the structure will be weak.

A Plumb Line to the Wall

An architect and a builder are looking over an old building when they notice that one wall is out of true, compared with the wall adjacent to it. 'I suppose one was built by an amateur and the other by a professional,' remarked the architect. 'I would say that both were built by professionals,' replies the builder, 'but one bricklayer used a plumb line and the other trusted his eye!' As we survey today that ancient building which calls itself 'the church' it is clear that over the centuries it has suffered at the hands of many professionals who have built 'by eye', and have never checked their work by the plumb line.

At a crucial point in the history of Israel God brought to the nation a solemn warning of impending judgement.

Amos was given a vision of the Lord standing by a wall with a plumb-line in his hand, and the message was: 'Look, I am setting a plumb-line among my people Israel; I will spare them no longer.'[27] Although this chapter may have special reference to leaders, it is needful for us all to know that God puts the plumb line of his word, not only to our personal lives, but also to that spiritual house of which we are part.

It is good to pause and ask ourselves how our local church measures up. Is it truly a community of God's people, like the New Testament churches? Or is it a mixed bag? Do the people, men and women, function as priests, offering up spiritual sacrifices in the assembly? Or is it more like a one-man band? Is each believer encouraged to discover his or her ministry, and given room to exercise it? Or is that the privilege of the favoured few? In a word, is your church a body of truly committed people, knitted and joined together, with each playing his individual role? Or are you carrying many spiritual passengers? The time has come for a radical assessment.

10

CHRIST AND TRADITION

Why is it that committed Christians, who bow to the authority of Scripture as far as their personal lives are concerned, have often great difficulty in submitting to that same rule when it comes to their church life? There may be ancillary answers, but the theme song of the popular musical *The Fiddler on the Roof* gives us the root answer—tradition. Tradition is strong because it is part and parcel of that granite structure, 'the establishment'. Strictly 'the establishment' means 'the ecclesiastical system established by law'; in this country, the Church of England. I am using it in the wider sense of every ecclesiastical system, ancient or modern, which produces a kind of conformity among its affiliated churches which we do not find in the churches of the New Testament.

It is not hoary antiquity alone that produces traditions. It is an attitude. Churches whose history does not span a century may have their own traditions which are as rigidly adhered to as any in the historic churches. 'Tradition or Scripture?' was a crucial issue in our Lord's confrontation with the religious authorities. It was a crucial issue in the Protestant reformation. It is no less a crucial issue today. But before we examine what our Lord had to say about it, let us look at his relationship in general with the religious authorities of his day.

Hated without a Cause

Jesus never came as a rabble-rouser or ranting revolutionary. It had been prophesied, 'He will not shout or cry out, or raise his voice in the streets.'[1] He was not a man with a chip on his shoulder, smarting under wrongs received, and determined to even the score by overthrowing the old order. God saw to it that his upbringing was orthodox. He was born under the law, circumcised the eighth day, in infancy presented in the temple, and in boyhood taken to Jerusalem for the Passover.

At thirty years of age he was still regularly attending the synagogue. He made it plain at the outset of his ministry that he had not come to abolish the law and the prophets but to fulfil them. He told a cleansed leper to show himself to the priest and offer the sacrifices that Moses had commanded. According to Jesus the teachers of the law, despite their hypocrisy, were to be obeyed.[2] Nevertheless there was a breach between Christ and the authorities almost from the outset of his ministry, a breach that grew wider with every week that passed.

Even if he had never criticized these leaders, everything about Jesus was calculated to antagonize them, simply because of who and what he was. There was a joy and freedom in his life-style that offended their religious asceticism. His attitude to eating and drinking they deemed wholly improper for a rabbi, so they dubbed him 'a glutton and a drunkard'. And as for the company he kept! How could he be from God and hobnob with tax collectors and other bad characters? He actually permitted a street girl to wash his feet with her tears and cover them with her kisses! Most grievous of all was the case of the woman they brought before him who had been caught in the act of adultery. The law required her to be stoned, but Jesus let her off scot-free, just a simple warning not to do it again! His was a radicalism that was expressed in mercy where there was true repentance.

The Striking Contrast

The authority with which Jesus taught and the mighty works that he performed could not have provided a more striking contrast with the sterile religion of the scribes and Pharisees. The positive response of the people to him hardly helped the situation. After a healing in the synagogue we read, 'All his opponents were humiliated, but the people were delighted with all the wonderful things he was doing.'[3] They flocked wherever he was, they hung on his words, while the wonders he performed were for ever 'the talk of the town'.

Towards the close of his ministry, when their opposition to him was coming to a head, they tried repeatedly to entangle him in his talk, and to trip him with their questions. But here was the galling thing, though they despised him as unlettered and unlearned, he won every debate, silenced them again and again, until at last they did not dare ask him another question. Is it any wonder that these religious leaders, totally destitute of the grace of God, were filled with envy and hatred, and could not rest until they had done away with him?

The Provocative Preacher

There is no doubt that Jesus was often intentionally provocative. To people with the strictest dietary rules over blood and meat, he said, 'Unless you eat the flesh of the Son of Man and drink his blood, you have no life in you.'[4] This caused many of his professed disciples to withdraw. Standing in the precincts of the temple, the nation's most sacred possession, he boldly declared, 'Destroy this temple, and I will raise it again in three days.'[5] And he never explained that he was referring to his body.

If only Jesus had not engaged in polemics. If only he had been content to live and let live. Why could he not have concentrated on the positive message he had to bring, and refrain from these outbursts against 'pious' men whose ways and words were different from his own? Simply because he was radical and knew that he was called to expose their 'piety' for what it was. Imagine an 'ordained' preacher, concluding his sermon with this tirade against the hierarchy of his denomination: 'You snakes! You brood of vipers! How will you escape being condemned to hell?'[6] The fact is that in those terrible words he was expressing the heart of God as truly as when he said to others, 'Come to me, all who are weary and burdened, and I will give you rest.'[7]

There was so much that Jesus had to say and to judge with regard to these leaders. He publicly warned his disciples of their pride, greed and religious ostentation.[8] He told them to beware of the yeast (meaning the teaching and influence) of the Pharisees which was hypocrisy.[9] From the outset of his ministry he stated publicly that unless men's righteousness surpassed that of the Pharisees and teachers of the law, they would never enter the kingdom of heaven. He had the audacity to preach 'without a licence' even within the sacred precincts of the temple. Right there, eyeball to eyeball, he told the chief priests and elders that the tax collectors and prostitutes would get into the kingdom of God before them.[10] No one was tempted to think that Jesus was aiming for the top of the denominational ladder!

The Traditions of the Elders

Since this whole question of what the Bible teaches about the church is beclouded by human tradition, it will be helpful to discover what Jesus had to say about traditions in his day. We find that the authorities were highly critical of him and his disciples because they did not observe the ceremonial washing before eating laid down by the scribes and Pharisees, nor their rigid and legalistic interpretation of the sabbath law.

In the New Testament the word 'tradition', or 'that which is handed down', is used in two quite distinct ways. Occasionally it refers to apostolic traditions which the churches were to obey.[11] This is straightforward, for apostolic tradition is thus equated with Scripture. But in most instances, and certainly on every occasion Jesus used the word, it refers to 'the traditions of men'—teachings that have been added to the word of God and handed down for the observance of succeeding generations.

In this second sense 'tradition' is sometimes used nowadays to refer to biblical interpretations or historic creeds and confessions which crystallize certain important doctrines. These must always be tested by Scripture. They have no authority for the Christian except as they truly express and elucidate what the Bible actually teaches. However, our primary concern is not with these, but with formularies or rules, relating to such matters as church order, ministry, services and rituals that are not based on Scripture. So often the only justification offered for a certain practice is: 'It is the tradition of our church.'

How Should We View Traditions?

Every responsible Christian needs to be fully persuaded in his own mind. Do we give it a place equal to Scripture, subordinate to Scripture, or no place at all? The Pharisees and scribes, though not the Sadducees, viewed their traditions as having equal authority with Scripture, believing that they had been passed down orally from Moses himself. Similarly, Catholics believe that their traditions have been passed down from the time of the apostles, and are therefore authoritative.

The Roman Catholic Church recognizes that the Bible is the word of God and that *tradition* is the word of the church. The

Council of Trent affirmed that *the deposit of faith was preserved in the Scriptures and in unwritten [i.e. extra-biblical] traditions, and that the Catholic Church accepts these two with equal devotion and reverence.*[12]

It is on this basis that they justify certain Catholic dogmas, such as 'the immaculate conception' and 'the assumption of Mary' which are not supported by Scripture.

Many evangelical Christians, who would have no sympathy for the Roman position, do accord tradition a real though subordinate place. John Stott takes the view that there were three important principles implicit in our Lord's teaching:

First, that Scripture is divine, while tradition is human. Secondly, that Scripture is obligatory, while tradition is optional. Thirdly, that Scripture is supreme, while tradition is subordinate.[13]

With regard to the washing of vessels and hands insisted on by the Pharisees he feels that hygienically it was quite a good idea, and ceremonially it was 'pretty harmless'. The only thing wrong was that the Pharisees made it obligatory. He also states:

Since Jesus neither justified nor rebuked his disciples' breach of the Pharisees' ritual tradition, this [quoting Edersheim] implied at least an attitude of indifference towards traditionalism.'[14]

In view of all the diverse and often contradictory traditions that litter the ecclesiastical scene, we need to check the facts.

Are Any Traditions Optional?

In the first place we must be clear whether 'obligatory' necessarily implies 'obligatory for salvation'. It is unlikely that the Pharisees taught that their traditions were obligatory for salvation, for they didn't seem to have any clear doctrine of salvation at all. Consider the rules that churches have formulated because they were thought to be necessary for the good order and discipline of the church. No rules are optional; they are made to be kept. In most churches those unordained are not usually permitted to baptize or lead in the administration of Holy Communion. This is not Scripture but tradition, but ministers and people are not expected to view the ruling as optional. In the Anglican communion a parish priest is not free to abandon the Prayer Book (or the Alternative Service Book) on a regular basis in favour of a non-liturgical service. If he does, tradition will soon make its presence felt.

Was Jesus Indifferent?

Is it true that the disciples' breach of the Pharisees' ritual tradition was neither justified nor rebuked by Jesus? Was his attitude one of indifference? Take the incident already referred to, where the Pharisees took Jesus to task for permitting his disciples to eat with unwashed hands.[15] Far from being a matter of 'indifference' to him, Jesus told them in no uncertain terms that their tradition was nullifying the word of God. He took up with them the command to honour one's father and mother. *'Moses said . . . but you say'* something quite different. The result of this is that a man is not permitted to obey the command of God. He is implying that their ritual washing was in the same category.

Jesus then made clear that their washing of hands was based on a complete misconception of the nature both of defilement and of cleansing. Eating with unwashed hands did not defile, and washing the hands did not ensure inner cleanliness. It was not what went in by way of food, but what came out by way of thoughts, words and deeds, that defiled a man. This 'harmless' ceremony was acting a falsehood, and consequently teaching a lie.

If Jesus had rebuked his disciples for eating with unwashed hands he would have rebuked them for following his own example, for he did the same when invited to dine with a Pharisee.[16] Common courtesy would have obliged him to fall in with 'the done thing' like the other guests, if his attitude had been neutral. In fact his attitude was one of studied non-observance, and in a room full of scribes and Pharisees that must have stuck out like a sore thumb. How strongly Jesus felt about this and other such traditions is clear from what follows.

He could so easily have left these religious leaders to draw their own conclusions from his failure to observe their tradition. He might have felt that his lips were sealed since he was the guest of a Pharisee. But this would not have been the reaction of a radical. Without further ado he launched a full-scale attack on the glaring unreality and hypocrisy he saw before him: 'Now then, you Pharisees clean the outside of cup and dish, but inside you are full of greed and wickedness.' And this was only the first broadside. He then uttered three woes on the Pharisees, and when a teacher of the law objected that he and his fellow lawyers were being implicated, he let them have a broadside too. If the guests ate at all they must have suffered from indigestion!

The Sabbath Tradition

When it came to the sabbath Jesus' attitude was no different. He kept the sabbath law, but ignored all the traditions that the Pharisees had added to the law, and this was a constant source of aggravation to them. Again he was eating in the house of a Pharisee, and they put a man suffering from dropsy in front of him to see what he would do. When they refused to answer his question as to whether it was lawful to heal on the sabbath or not, he took the man and healed him anyway.

The Pharisees viewed plucking ears of corn and rubbing them in the hand a mini-form of reaping and threshing, and therefore quite unlawful on the sabbath. Jesus would have known this and could have counselled his disciples not to antagonize the Pharisees unnecessarily. Not only did he *not* do so, but when they questioned him about it he used the Scriptures to show how wrong they were in their observance of the sabbath law.

It was the same with the man in the synagogue with a withered hand. He knew they were watching him. He could have whispered, 'Come round to where I am staying tomorrow morning and I'll heal you then.' To Jesus it was not a situation that called for tact and diplomacy. Their traditions involved a false concept of spirituality which he met head on and exposed for what it was.

Where Adding Means Subtracting

You could say that the Pharisees with their traditions *added* to the word of God, while the Sadducees with their unbelief in the resurrection and the supernatural *subtracted* from it. But it is important to see that adding of this kind always results in subtracting. This should be clear once we see that the Bible is not only supreme but *sufficient*. Add to what is complete and you take from it. Salvation illustrates this. When men add their own good deeds and piety to Christ's finished work on the cross, they do not enhance it, they detract from it. They are virtually saying, 'This complete work is not really complete, it needs my contribution.' Hence Jesus told the Pharisees, 'You have *let go* of the commands of God and are *holding on* to the traditions of men.'[17] This is a case where holding on always results in letting go. In the house of the Pharisee he told the scribes, 'Woe to you experts in the law, because you have *taken away the key to knowledge*.'[18] He was referring to the Scriptures. They had taken them away from men by all the traditions they had introduced. Traditions still do, and that is why we cannot adopt an attitude of indifference.

Were the Reformers Radical?

We have already noted that tradition was a major issue in the reformation. While Rome insisted that ecclesiastical traditions had equal authority with the Bible, the watchword of the reformers was *sola scriptura*—Scripture alone. They insisted that nothing outside of it was needed for salvation, and it was the canon by which all traditions were to be judged. So far so good, but the question is: did the reformers go far enough?

God has not only spoken in his word about salvation and Christian living, he has given us principles concerning the ordering of our corporate life, and spoken of the composition and function of the Christian community, as I have shown in these last two chapters. It seems, however, that the reformers were unwilling to extend their conviction concerning *the sufficiency of Scripture* beyond the question of salvation.

> Luther and the confessions... viewed the written tradition of the fathers as useful for interpreting the scripture but not as a source or norm of teaching.... The attitude of Luther and the confessions was conservative, they retained whatever did not conflict with the gospel of justification through faith.[19]

This non-radical attitude of the reformers left many unscriptural traditions untouched, needing to be challenged by restoration movements of the Spirit in the centuries to follow.

Where God Has Spoken

In these chapters I have sought to show that God has declared his mind concerning his church. He has said, be it in embryo, all that needs to be said. Room for elaboration, elucidation, interpretation and application, yes, but for addition, no. *Sola scriptura!* The word is enough. Traditions that add to it only take from it. They deny its sufficiency. They rob it of its effectiveness. They do to the church what the traditions of the scribes and Pharisees did to true spirituality in the time of Christ.

What the church is saying through its traditions is, 'God has not made it clear in the Bible, so we will make it clear for all succeeding generations.' Or they are saying, 'What the Bible has to say may have been adequate for the primitive church, but we have moved on since then. Changing situations and problems demand new measures.' In other words, God was a little short-sighted when he inspired the New Testament writers.

When Jesus spoke about the inability of the old wineskin to contain the new wine, his parable had direct application to Judaism. The weakness of an old wineskin is that it is inflexible, and we have seen that the major cause of Judaistic inflexibility was tradition. But the principle still holds. Churches locked in tradition are old wineskins, and the Spirit of God is seriously limited in what he is able to do. When we move from traditional churches to New Testament churches we move from rigidity, uniformity and complexity to flexibility, variety and simplicity. T. C. Hammond, writing on the nature of the church, does well to remind us:

The church is an organism rather than an organisation. It is for this reason that elaborate instructions, comparable with those of Leviticus, are absent in the New Testament. Much latitude is left for national or local differences, and *uniformity is not enjoined....The rules for the church are found to be a series of*

*principles.... The distinguishing features of the apostolic eccle-
siastical traditions are simplicity and adaptability.*[20]

We Have Lost Something

After months studying and translating the Acts of the
Apostles another celebrated Anglican records how the
experience left him 'profoundly stirred and, to be honest,
disturbed'. The following three extracts are taken from
J. B. Phillips' preface to his translation of the Acts.

> We cannot help feeling disturbed as well as moved, for this
> surely is *the church as it was meant to be*. It is vigorous and
> flexible, for these are the days before it ever became fat and
> short of breath through prosperity, or muscle-bound by over-
> organisation. These men did not make 'acts of faith', they
> believed; they did not 'say their prayers', they really prayed.
> They did not hold conferences on psychosomatic medicine,
> they simply healed the sick. But if they were uncomplicated
> and naive by modern standards we have ruefully to admit that
> they were *open on the Godward side* in a way that is almost
> unknown today....

> In the pages of this unpretentious book (the Acts of the
> apostles) the fresh air of heaven is plainly blowing, and to turn
> from the vitality of these pages to almost any current Christian
> writing, be it a theological book or a church periodical, is to
> bring tears to Christian eyes. *Of course the moment one suggests
> that our tragically-divided and tradition-choked church might
> learn from this early unsophistication, one is accused of over-
> simplification of the issues involved in our modern world.* But it
> should be remembered that the ancient world was not without
> its complex problems also. It is of course possible that the
> translator has had his head turned by too close a study of these
> artless and energetic pages, but nevertheless he feels after
> such study that the Holy Spirit has a way of short-circuiting
> human problems. Indeed, *in exactly the same way as Jesus
> Christ in the flesh cut right through the matted layers of tradition
> and exposed the real issue;* just as he again and again brought

down a real problem to a personal issue, so we find the Spirit of
Jesus dealing not so much with problems as with people . . . .

Of course it is easy to 'write off' this little history of the church's
first beginnings as simply an account of an enthusiastic but
ill-regulated and unorganised adolescence, to be followed by a
well-disciplined maturity in which embarrassing irregularities
no longer appear. But this is surely too easy an explanation
altogether. *We in the modern church have unquestionably lost
something.* Whether it is due to a stifling churchiness, whether
it is due to our sinful complacency over the scandal of a divided
church, or whatever the cause may be, very little of the modern
church could bear comparison with the spiritual drive, the
genuine fellowship, and the gay unconquerable courage of the
Young Church.[21]

We have lost something all right, there is no doubt about
that. But the vital questions are, What have we lost? And
why?

The Church as It Was Meant to Be

Let us turn from the stuffy atmosphere of traditional
Christianity to where 'the fresh air from heaven is plainly
blowing', and see if we can find out what we have lost.
Using inspired glimpses the Holy Spirit gives us in the
pages of the New Testament, a pinch of sanctified imagi-
nation plus a little oriental flavouring, let us visit 'the
church as it was meant to be'.

We find ourselves in a city in a Roman province of Asia.
We enquire of a passing stranger if he can tell us 'where
the Christians meet'. To our great joy we are speaking to a
deacon of the church, Timotheus by name. Discovering
we too are believers he greets us with a holy kiss, and then
conducts us to the place of meeting.

'Our congregation has only two hundred believers, but
the church in the city is nearer two thousand,' he explains

as we walk along. 'It began when our brother Paul visited this province five years ago. That was when I was converted. At first we were only a handful of believers, but now the work has grown rapidly.'

We ask about the leadership, and about his own role as a deacon. The congregation has five elders. Two of these are men who give themselves wholly to the ministry, while the others have secular employment. The senior one among them, Artemas, is not only a shepherd and teacher, but sometimes travels with brother Paul. Yes, there are several deacons beside himself who serve the church in a great variety of ways. His own role is caring for the poor and the widows in the community.

At last we have arrived at the place of meeting, to find people converging from all directions. The believers all place their tithes and offerings in a large receptacle near the door. We notice a little woman with wizened face lay some home-made cheese beside the offering box for the poor. 'She is a widow,' explains Timotheus. 'We do not know how she is able to give so generously.' We hardly notice the buzz of conversation as the saints greet one another, or the noise of people finding their places in the assembly. There is an awareness of God in this place which produces a right kind of reverence and a holy expectation in the people.

We look around. What a cross-section! There are Jews and Gentiles, slaves and free, young and old, rich and poor, all mingling freely and without distinction. We have only to see the way they greet each other to know that these Christians really do love each other. An elder at the front with a strong melodious voice commences to sing a psalm. Instantly the buzz of conversation ceases, and the congregation takes up the singing. 'One thing have I desired of the Lord, that will I seek after, that I may dwell in the house of the Lord all the days of my life. *To behold the beauty of the Lord and to enquire in his temple.*'

They sing those last words over and over, like a refrain—'to behold the beauty of the Lord and to enquire in his temple' —until they seem to be burned into everyone's spirit.

As the psalm ends a man at the front playing a lyre commences a hymn which is sung through several times. Other songs follow. Then two sing to one another responsively. 'The Lord is a man of war, the Lord of Hosts is his name,' comes from someone standing near us. Then from the other side comes an answering voice, 'Let God arise and let his enemies be scattered.' Then the first singer again, 'And we will go forth with him, to share the spoils of victory'—and so on. This inspired singing seems to ignite the worship and the whole company is then caught up in spiritual singing, some in their native tongue, some in their unknown tongue, and despite ourselves we are caught up too. We have never heard anything like this before—harmony without melody—swelling to a glorious crescendo, with the people breaking out in spontaneous applause—and then dying away to a whisper, as though controlled by some unseen conductor.

We look about us. As well as great joy and exuberant praise there is an awe of God here. A middle-aged woman not far from us, eyes shut, hands raised, is lost in the worship of her God. Then our eyes are riveted by the face of a young man. 'Only last week he was an idolater,' whispers Timotheus. His face is ecstatic with joy. This must be what Peter meant by 'joy unspeakable and full of glory'.

There is a pause in the continuous flow of worship. An elderly man with the unmistakable features of a Jew rises to pray. His hands and eyes are lifted heavenward. His speech is simple, but he knows how to touch the throne of God. He prays for the Emperor, for local rulers, for the nation, and for the word of God to prosper. Hardly is he through when a young man is on his feet, praying fervently for the progress of the gospel in the city, that every believer will witness boldly, that God will stretch out his hand to heal, and that signs and wonders may be done in Jesus' name.

At this a man breaks in with a testimony. For some time he had been trying to share the good news with his parents, apparently without success, but this past week his father was seized with a raging fever, and fearing he was going to die he had rebuked the sickness in Jesus' name and his father had been healed. 'My parents are here,' he continues, pointing to the elderly couple beside him; 'they now want to hear about the Way.' Spontaneous applause and shouts of 'Hallelujah' greet the news, followed by another wave of praise. There are further prayers, for imprisoned saints, for those suffering persecution, and for the testimony in other parts. There are utterances in tongues, each followed by interpretation in the form of inspired prayer or praise. There are visions, revelations and prophecies bringing simple words of exhortation and encouragement.

It seems that 'everyone has a hymn, or a word of instruction, a revelation, a tongue or an interpretation'. All are evidently free to participate as the Spirit leads, the men with heads bared, the women with heads (but not faces) veiled. We are just thinking that a company so spiritual hardly needs leaders whan a man stands up to speak of a grievance he has with another brother. A voice from the front interrupts him: 'We have not come to hear about your grievances, brother.' 'I was only trying to explain,' persists the brother. Now there is a ring of authority about the voice from the front: 'Brother Hermas, I command you to sit down.' Meekly brother Hermas complies. 'That was Artemas, the brother that works with Paul,' whispers the deacon.

The rebuke has subdued the meeting. We turn again to Timotheus: 'Are your meetings always like this?' 'No,' he whispers, 'they are never like this, they are always different. You never quite know—' He lapses into silence as a clear strong voice comes from the front: 'I am calling my people to a time of great enlargement—enlargement of heart, of faith and of vision. I have still very many in this city that sit in darkness. The fields are waiting to be harvested. Go and bring in the sheaves. There will be opposition and persecution, but do not fear the roaring of the lion. I will be with you to give you success.' This is the gist of an utterance that lasts some few minutes.

Artemas is on his feet. 'Let us weigh carefully the words of the prophet,' he says quietly. 'Let it sink into our hearts. I am confident this is God's word to us now. It is wholly in keeping with what God has given me to say.' He looks down at a scroll in his hand. 'These are words written by brother Paul to the believers in Philippi.' He reads the whole epistle, pausing here and there to explain words or phrases that the uneducated believers would find difficult to understand. He then takes up the theme of joy in the midst of tribulation. This joy would be their strength. It would prove irresistible. Through faith and prayer they would triumph and reap the promised harvest. The people wait on his words, as a starving man reaches out his hand for bread. It is a powerful and practical message, and each telling point draws responses of approval from the eager listeners.

The teaching ends, but before dismissing the assembly Artemas calls for 'brother Cassius'. A Roman in his mid-thirties makes his way somewhat nervously to the front to face the congregation. Sadly the leader tells the church that this brother has fallen into sin with a woman outside the church. One can feel the shock waves hitting the people, and leaving behind the sound of a deep sigh. 'This is a grievous sin, which wounds us all,' continues the leader with tears in his eyes. 'Though we thank God the relationship has been broken, until the elders are satisfied that there has been genuine repentance our brother will attend the meetings but not participate in them, nor will he share in the Supper of the Lord.' Many are in tears as Cassius returns, white and shaken, to his place.

Artemas continues. 'I have been asked by the presbytery to announce that brother Rufus from the Patrias congregation is under discipline for being a trouble-maker in several congregations. We shall not receive him here, and you are not to receive him into your homes. If he comes to you, tell him to return to the elders of his congregation and put things right. That is all. Grace, mercy and peace be with you.' The meeting is over. We can hardly believe that over three hours have passed. They have gone like a dream.

'What did Artemas mean by "the presbytery"?' we ask Timotheus.

'That is the body of elders that rule the whole church in the city,' he replies. 'Artemas is the only elder in our congregation who belongs to the city presbytery. They deal with any difficulties between congregations, and decide when the whole church should come together. These are the leaders brother Paul always meets with when he comes to the city.'

'We noticed that the congregation prayed for churches in other cities. There must be many in this province alone. Governing and administering these must be an enormous task. Where is your—er—denominational headquarters?'

'I beg your pardon.'

'Do you not have some central governing body?'

'If there is I haven't heard about it. We are linked with the other churches in the region through the travelling ministers, our brother Paul, and those in the apostolic team that he leads. They move round the churches and bring teaching and apostolic direction as may be needed.'

'Before we go, please tell us, when is the next meeting?'

Timotheus smiles. 'In a way we are meeting all the time. What you have seen this morning is only one aspect of our community life. We like to share our lives as much as possible, and serve each other in practical ways. That's what we understand by 'fellowship'. Most of our meetings are in homes, where we share meals as well as break bread together.'

We thank our brother warmly and bid him farewell with some feeling of sadness. Then we slip out into the noise and bustle of this oriental city with a lot to think about.

To say that we have 'lost something' would be an understatement. Not only variety, simplicity and flexibility, but even more important, a certain quality of faith and spirituality.

The Final Brief

And if we are honest we must acknowledge that traditions have had a big part to play in it. There are inevitably those who are unconcerned. They say, 'Let's get on with the business of living the Christian life and saving souls.' That is about as realistic as the lumberman who says 'I've no time to sharpen my axe. I'm much too busy felling trees.' At the risk of some repetition, here is my brief against ecclesiastical traditions:

1. They tend to obscure or nullify the word of God. We have spoken of the clergy/laity dichotomy which nullifies the biblical principle of the priesthood of all believers, and infant baptism which obscures and confuses the whole purpose of the ordinance. If it were not bolstered by tradition infant baptism would fall over without being knocked, so devoid is it of clear scriptural support.

2. They put a yoke on the neck of disciples, and especially on their corporate worship, which produces bondage. Liturgies and fixed forms of service—whether the Prayer Book variety, the 'hymn-and-a-thing-hymn-and-a-thing' of Non-Conformity, or even the unvarying pattern that many charismatic groups have unconsciously adopted— militate against our being able to 'worship by the Spirit of

God'.[22] Liturgies, whether ancient or modern, written or unwritten, are a human device, to keep the religious wheels turning by doing what is customary, rather than exercising faith in the immediate presence and operation of the Spirit. Consequently they cover up the need for the return of the Spirit when he has departed, and they hinder faith for spontaneity and variety.

3. They stumble and confuse believers who do not have discernment to distinguish between that which God requires of them according to Scripture, and that which men require of them according to tradition.

4. They keep us in our denominational boxes, despite all our talk about unity, and this is a stumbling block to the world which is not offset by united evangelism. Inter-denominational fellowship is a poor substitute for the unity that God is after.

5. They greatly restrict the flow of the Spirit. The church becomes like a furred-up water pipe. You turn on the shower and all you get is a dribble.

6. They prevent the full deployment of all the gifts and graces resident in the body of Christ, so that gifted men and women look for outlets in para-church organizations, to the weakening of the church.

7. They deprive the church of her spiritual flexibility to cope with all the new things God is wanting to do.

8. They render the church an ineffective instrument for world evangelism, so that the brunt of this task is left to para-church organizations, which can never be as effective as God's chosen means—local churches, church-based evangelists, and church-based apostolic teams.

9. They prevent the people of God coming individually and corporately to full maturity, 'the measure of the stature of the fullness of Christ', in preparation for Christ's return.

10. In a word, they are totally counter-productive when it comes to those declared purposes that God is out to accomplish through the church.

Where Do We Go From Here?

Perhaps you belong to a traditional church, and have therefore found this chapter quite disturbing. You are wondering what are the practical implications of what I have been saying for people like you. Is this all leading up to a 'Come out' call? We must reserve the answer to that for the next chapter.

11

DENOMINATIONAL DILEMMA

It was early in the seventies that many Christians from traditional backgrounds who had received the Holy Spirit found themselves facing ostracism and opposition in their churches. Some left to form new groups or to join churches where the attitude was more sympathetic. There was much debate on what came to be known as the 'stay in/ come out' controversy. It was raised in conferences and discussed in magazines. Both then and since, the charismatic renewal has issued an uncompromising call to all church waverers, dissidents or potential deserters—'Stay in your church,' at least as much as in you lies. If you get thrown out join some other established church, but do not form a new church. That would be to miss God's best.

As one quite deeply involved in the charismatic movement from the start I sounded a different note. I said that any unqualified calls either to 'stay in' or 'come out' were equally mistaken. 'To do this without knowing what God may be saying to the individual is to be guilty of presumption, and of usurping the prerogative of the Holy Spirit.'[1] One is failing to make any allowance for personal conscience or conviction. Those who issue 'blanket' calls of this sort would do well to ask themselves what their real motive is. Is it the spiritual good of the individual? Or is it the support and preservation of the institution of which they are a part? Or with others, the increase of 'the new thing' to which they are committed?

It is not easy to discuss objectively and dispassionately the question of denominational affiliation. All the sworn enemies of New Testament radicalism—sentiment, custom, tradition—come baying around us. In the first place people only have foggy ideas about the nature of the church. There is conflict over denominational loyalty. People are torn by a sense of gratitude and obligation to a minister who has been used to their blessing. They have church involvements and commitments. They are influenced by family tradition, by friends, by sentimental attachment to a building, and to their religious past. There is a security in clinging to the known rather than stepping out into the unknown, and much else. Ministers have additional anxiety over their livelihood and place of abode. Though these are formidable factors, to the radical Christian *not one of them, nor even all of them put together,* will determine this issue. They do not touch the root of the matter.

The Remnant Doctrine

Leaders within historic churches are often very frank in admitting that 'the formal established church (of any denomination) is irrelevant, formal, stuffy, dead,' and a positive hindrance in evangelism. Nevertheless they feel they should stay put and 'look for renewal from within'. The argument from Scripture usually used to support this position is 'the remnant doctrine'. This view holds that Israel, despite her terrible backslidings, was never finally overthrown by God. Instead he worked through a godly remnant within the nation, through prophets and leaders, to bring back the people to himself. Likewise our Lord came as a root out of dry ground. He did not split away from the dead religious tradition of his day but attended the synagogue and the temple.

It is certainly true that God uses a remnant to revive and restore his people, but that which corresponds to Israel as a nation in the Old Testament is now the church, the body of Christ, not a denomination of christendom. This is where so many arguments come unstuck. There is a tacit assumption that 'churches' which may be completely devoid of spiritual life are to be equated with 'the body of Christ', and that to come out of such is to divide that body.

The idea that God bears indefinitely with an apostate people is not true. Jesus informed the Jews of his day that the kingdom had in fact been taken from them, and given to a nation (the church) producing its fruit.[2] It is true that he stayed with 'the establishment', but not to the bitter end. There came for him 'the point of no return' when he concluded his denunciation of the religious leaders with these solemn words: 'Your house is left to you desolate.... You will not see me again until you say, "Blessed is he who comes in the name of the Lord."'[3]

It is not surprising, therefore, that after Pentecost Jesus' followers, though they attended synagogue and temple until they got thrown out, established separate communities, the churches of the New Testament. In the parables of the tattered garment and the brittle wineskin, which we considered earlier, Jesus had already taught them that he had not come to do a *renewal* job on Israel, but a *replacement* job. The kingdom had been transferred. 'The new thing' was now the remnant, and the nucleus of what was to come. Is it not conceivable that God's remnant today may also be 'a new thing' outside 'the establishment'?

According to the remnant doctrine Paul ought to have stayed within 'the establishment' and worked for change from within. In fact the inevitable result of his conversion was the very opposite, as D. A. Hubbard points out:

Almost nothing in the apostle's life illustrates so clearly the radical change wrought by his conversion than the dramatic reversal in his relationship to the priestly establishment. The beginning of his story found him riding with the hounds; the end, running with the foxes.[4]

Denominational Loyalty

Provided a believer is convinced that his membership of a local church is in the will of God he should always be encouraged to be loyal to that local body of believers. But often, behind the 'stay-in' call, there is something more than this—an appeal for denominational loyalty. Since denominations have no biblical basis we are skating on thin ice when we appeal for that kind of loyalty. The vast majority of those who own allegiance to historic denominations do so, not because of biblical convictions, but because that was the tradition in which they were brought up. My wife's parents happened to be nominal Anglicans, and this was the reason why she was christened, confirmed and reared an Anglican.

To those of us outside 'the establishment' it seems contradictory for those within it to speak of it as an 'irrelevant, formal, stuffy, dead' institution, and at the same time make such a vigorous appeal for people to stay within it at all costs. Do people really believe that it is as bad as they say? Or is there a deeper reason for this extraordinary counsel? I believe the major reason is to be found in the previous chapter. It is motivated by traditionalism rather than New Testament radicalism. Behind such thinking is a tacit assumption that a certain validity, even sanctity attaches to the old that the new doesn't possess. Scripture gives no support whatsoever to the notion that there is anything sacrosanct about traditional structures.

'Out of the Frying Pan into . . .'?

An oft-repeated argument in favour of staying with a denominational church is that any new thing that you join will in due course become an old thing, form itself into another denomination, and you are back where you started.

> Countless Christian groups have split away from some tradi-
> tional denomination with every intention of forming a 'pure'
> church. For a time all is well...but before long the same
> pattern emerges: purity becomes impurity, vitality becomes
> formality, orthodoxy becomes hypocrisy. And the Christian
> landscape is further polluted with yet another 'denomination'
> to confuse the world.[1]

No doubt all will be agreed that denominations pollute the Christian landscape and confuse the world. But the idea that people leave their denominations to form a 'pure church' could be misleading. Initially it may have more to do with 'foundation' than with 'purity'. Those who attempt to justify the mixture in the churches of christendom have inevitably followed Calvin and used Corinth as a whipping boy. If gross evils, so the argument goes, such evils as are not found in nominal churches today, could exist in Corinth, and it still be recognized by Paul as a true church, how can anyone argue for a 'pure church' today?

We must distinguish here two things which are being confused. Though Corinth wasn't 'a pure church', it did possess a true foundation. It was composed of true believers, however carnal. We need to remember that they were new converts from a background of gross idolatry and immorality, and not be too harsh in our judgement of them. Paul wasn't. Just read through the two Corinthian letters looking for the positive things Paul has to say. You will be surprised at how much he could commend—far more than when he wrote to the much more 'respectable' Galatians. Because Corinth was on a proper foundation its condition could be dealt with. Because traditional churches are not on such a foundation, but locked into unbiblical structures, they are difficult if not impossible to correct. When dealing with a biblical structure the New Testament will provide us with guidelines for its establishment, its function and its adjustment. But with a traditional structure one is at sea without chart or compass.

Are Break-Away Movements Always Wrong?

Let us assume for a moment that the premiss is true, that every new move out of a traditional structure will in due course revert to type and turn denominational, and ask ourselves whether that provides a sound reason for not getting involved. We need to be reminded that all the major denominations in the west, except for the Roman Catholic Church, are the result of break-away movements. If none had ever taken place we would all, including the Anglican Church, be under Mother Rome, one big denomination. Most of us are very thankful that that is not the position. Handley Moule has this significant explanation of such movements:

> In almost every great instance of secession from the main organisation it will be found that part of the cause was the neglect, or repression, of some great principle of life or order on the part of the main body of its representative authorities.[5]

To put it differently, these secessions were great recovery movements, being part of the grand strategy of heaven to restore the church to New Testament Christianity, and the end is not yet. Think of a few of the great truths that had been lost to the medieval church, but which have been restored to us by much maligned break-away movements:

Justification by faith apart from any meritorious works.
Practical holiness.
Baptism of believers by immersion.

Priesthood of all believers and congregational partici-
pation.
Plurality of elders ruling the local church.
Baptism in the Spirit and spiritual gifts for today.
And much else.

We should thank God for every break-away movement
that has recovered to the church something she had lost,
even though that movement deteriorated, became a
denominational structure, and her early glory departed.

Apart from all this there have been innumerable revivals
that have deeply blessed the church, but which have not
involved any reformation of church structure or departure
from the parent body. They have resulted in a harvest of
conversions as well as the reviving of God's people. But
these have usually declined more swiftly than the other
sort. Invariably within a few years the revival needed
reviving. Because the spiritual temperature fell and the
churches involved settled back into their normal routine,
that did not mean that all the fruit was forfeited, or that
the revival was a big mistake. There seems no more
reason in this argument than that of a man who says that
he doesn't want to get rid of his old car that is on its last
legs, because all new cars have a perverse tendency to
grow old!

Is Denominationalizing Inevitable?

Is every 'new thing' that God produces doomed to go the
way of all flesh? Are we to accept that God has sentenced
his church to a denominational merry-go-round to the end
of time? Is there a gravitational pull, a kind of law of
perpetual decline, that makes any effort to jump clear a
futile exercise?

Such a view cannot go unchallenged. It is too much like
the philosophy of life put forward by 'the Preacher in
Jerusalem':

Generations come and generations go, but the earth remains for ever. The sun rises and the sun sets, and hurries back to where it rises. The wind blows to the south and turns to the north; round and round it goes, ever returning on its course. All streams flow into the sea, yet the sea is never full. To the place the streams come from, there they return again. All things are wearisome, more than one can say.[6]

In other words, there may be movements and processes, but they all end up where they started. 'Nothing changes here.' That may be true of the physical world, but we simply cannot go along with such an hypothesis in relation to God's people, not if we have ever caught a vision of the restored church in the pages of the New Testament. How can we speak in one breath of 'the scandal of a divided church', or the Christian landscape being polluted by denominations, and then suggest that this is how it must remain to the end of time? This neither accords with the character of God nor with the prophetic Scriptures.

What Are You Believing for?

Before anyone settles for a permanently divided church let him face honestly what it really means:

1. That despite exhorting his church to preserve 'the unity of the Spirit', and to mature till it reaches 'unity in the faith',[7] God has in fact given up all hope of the church ever getting it together. He is resigned to his people being denominationally segmented till the end of the age, although that was never in his plan.

2. That the prayer of Jesus, 'that all of them may be *one*, Father, *just as you are in me and I am in you*...that they may be *one as we are one*,'[8] is never going to be fulfilled till Jesus comes back. The nature of this unity for which Jesus prayed is not compatible with a church denominationally divided.

3. This means that the prayer of Jesus that they may be

brought to complete unity *so that the world may believe'* is nullified, for when Jesus comes it will be too late for the world to believe.

4. That the return of the Bridegroom for a glorious Bride who has made herself ready for her Husband[9] means in fact Christ returning for a dislocated unprepared Bride still in her innumerable denominational boxes, with her many differences still unresolved.

5. That instead of this event being the glorious climax of the age, it will be a tragic anti-climax, with the people of God not even attaining to the measure of unity they enjoyed in the first century, when at least there were no denominational divisions.

It may well be argued that the denominational view has got history on its side. That is true, but this opposing view has got *the purpose of God and the prayer of Jesus* on its side. God is bigger than past history. His future purposes cannot be limited by past events.

I remember as a small boy being asked a simple conundrum. A snail climbing a six-foot wall covered two feet each day and slipped back one foot each night. How long did it take to climb the wall? I fell for the catch, and said, 'Six days.' I had failed to recognize that on the fifth and last day there was advance, but no slipping back. The vision of the restoration of the church calls for a final phase of church history when there will be advance to final consummation, and no slipping back. Does that concept stretch God beyond his measure? Or is it just too much for our faith?

The Bogey of Division

Whenever in the history of the church God has done something new the cry of 'Division!' has come from the die-hards. It's like a spiritual burglar alarm warning the faithful that someone or something is getting in that ought not to be allowed. It was a widespread cry in the early days of the charismatic movement. It is heard today when mention is made of someone leaving his church. There is a prevailing idea that division is always an unmitigated evil. This is not the case. Division may indeed be a work of the devil, but it may also be a weapon in God's armoury. It is not necessarily the enemy of unity. It may in the end effect the kind of unity we all desire.

It is a sad but inescapable fact of spiritual experience that truth divides. The truth of the gospel divides families, husband from wife and parents from children. It divides those who receive from those who reject. The truth concerning water baptism and Spirit baptism divides one believer from another. 'We used to have good fellowship with you until you embraced this pentecostal teaching.' Many of us have felt the hurt when such remarks have come from those we loved and respected. But we could not deny what we had come to believe and experience, not even to preserve a valued friendship. We pay too high a price for unity if it costs us the truth.

When people leave their churches because they are following convictions which they believe God has given them, let us not be swift to accuse them of being divisive, not at least till we know all the facts. If we do *we* may be the ones who are grieving the Holy Spirit. There are times when God himself takes the initiative to bring division and disturbance into situations. I read of a New Testament church in the USA where God was manifestly moving. Accusations were flying around—'They're dividing the body...stealing the sheep...disturbing the unity... becoming a cult.' It was God who spoke into their midst: 'You are not disturbing the unity, but you are disturbing the status quo.' There are too many status quos around that need disturbing. Every move of the Holy Spirit is a move of the Holy Disturber.

Not Peace but a Sword

When God shatters our peace and unity by the moving of his Spirit it usually means that our peace and unity is shallow and superficial. The little world of Judaism of that first century was relatively peaceful till Jesus stepped into it. He didn't come with an olive branch but with a sword. He didn't come with a call to unity but with a message that he knew would divide the nation. And he did not hesitate to announce the fact:

> I did not come to bring peace, but a sword.[10]
> I have come to bring fire on the earth.[11]
> Do you think I came to bring peace on earth? No, I tell you, but division.[12]

Of course Jesus wanted to bring peace and unity, but first the sword, the word that went forth from his mouth, had to do its work. It would pierce, dividing soul and spirit, joints and marrow. It would cleave through the unreality and religiosity of the day, dividing the true from the false, the wheat from the chaff, and laying bare the thoughts and motives of men's hearts. Jesus and his kingdom message would be a touchstone of faith and character, and that which would determine the destinies of men.

Our divided christendom does not need another call to unity. It needs the coming of 'the sword' that will slay all our futile efforts to patch the unpatchable and join the unjoinable. We need an incisive word that will confront the professing church with the government of God. Not just a word for the traditional church-goer, but one that will also smite the hearts of evangelicals, pentecostals and charismatics. Some will respond and some will resist, but all will have the thoughts of their hearts revealed. Only 'the sword' can cleave a path to bring in the true unity of the church.

I see no future for denominations because I don't find them in the heavenly blue-print. They are contrary to God's declared purpose for his church in this age. But I do see a glorious future for the people of God, many of whom are currently in denominations. There are some reading these pages who should leave the churches with which they are associated, and need to seek God earnestly as to where he would have them planted. Equally, there are others who may want to move but should be counselled to stay where they are. Here are a few guiding principles.

Stay Put...

1. ...When the spirit of the persons wanting to leave is wrong. Those with a bitter or rebellious spirit towards their former leaders need to be sent back and told to submit to their leaders and get their spirit right. At the close of a house meeting in Devon a Pentecostal lady remarked to me,

'If my pastor knew I was here I'd be in trouble.'

'How is that?' I asked.

'He has forbidden us to attend any meetings of the house church movement.'

'What, then, are you doing here?' I asked.

'Oh,' she replied, 'I come for the spiritual food. It's such a blessing.'

I told her that if she was a committed member of a Pentecostal church she should obey those who were over her in the Lord, as the word of God commands.

2. ...When the motivation for leaving is simply boredom with the old, or like the Athenians, to be involved in 'some new thing'. Instead of 'sermon-tasters' we now have 'church-tasters'. Like bumble bees they flit from flower to flower, thinking to settle on the one that takes their fancy. They need to know where they belong and 'bloom where they're planted'.

3. ...When church affiliation is ruled by convenience or expedience. Such people are completely in the dark as to the principles governing New Testament church life, so that whatever their reasons for wanting to move they fall short of the one thing needful—biblical conviction.

Come Out...

1. ...If a believer is in what purports to be a church, but the members are nominal and the minister gives no evidence of having the life of God. The believer should leave his religious club and find a church, a true community of God's people. By pulling out he is no more dividing the body of Christ than if he resigned from the Rotary Club or the Freemason's Lodge.

2. ...If the believer's conscience is troubled by doctrines or practices in the church to which he belongs which he knows to be unscriptural. If he is stifling his conscience he is grieving the Holy Spirit and his spiritual life will suffer.

3. ...If to stay where he is would involve a practical denial of spiritual truth and experience which has become part and parcel of his Christian life. How many genuinely blessed in the Spirit through the charismatic renewal have dried up, and virtually lost whatever they had received, because they stayed with a church which, if it did not openly *deny* it, certainly *discouraged* their experience. If they were advised, 'Stay put regardless,' those who gave such counsel must be prepared to share the blame for their resultant spiritual state.

4. ...If a believer's supreme ambition is to press on with God, but he finds himself constantly frustrated by his church setting. For example, if the teaching is not meeting his need and the church does not provide a milieu in which the gifts God has given him can develop and he himself can come to maturity, he would be well advised to ask himself and God, Is this really where I am planted?

This last situation allows the possibility that God may require the believer to stay put and hold on in faith for significant change. But if after a reasonable period there is no change, and he is not really in faith for that, he should be ready to move. Before any believer moves it is only honourable to share with the pastor or church leaders fully and honestly the reasons for his decision.

Moving on with God

As we have already said, truth divides. The truth concerning the New Testament church divides believers who are determined to enter into what God has shown them from those who do not consider it a matter of importance and prefer to stay where they are and just get on with the job. This is a major reason why the movement called 'the charismatic renewal' is declining fast in the USA and the UK.

The one essential of a movement of the Spirit is that it keeps moving. The charismatic renewal moved in faith and obedience to possess its inheritance in the baptism and gifts of the Holy Spirit. Then came the challenge to shaky church structures that were not adequate to contain and utilize the gifts that God was giving. It was a challenge to radical reformation and recovery, a casting out of what did not belong and a building of walls that had been broken down. Important as was the recovery of spiritual gifts, it was only one step towards the restoration of the church to New Testament Christianity. There was much more to come, but the charismatic renewal cried, 'Halt!' Leaders were not willing for what was involved.

There were, however, those who were determined to press on regardless. The ironical thing is that they are the ones who are looked upon as being out of line, and accused of dividing the body of Christ. In the Israelites' desert journeyings God led the way by the pillar of cloud.

When it hovered they encamped, and when it moved they journeyed. Let us imagine that the cloud leads them to a pleasant oasis and there tarries awhile. When at length it moves there is a division in the camp. The majority feel that they have journeyed far enough. They refuse to move on. The rest pack their bags and move with the cloud. Who would you think was to blame for the split?

We must continue to move because the cloud is still moving. If we stop we stagnate. If we crystallize we shall soon fossilize. The hour of destiny in which we live calls for men and women of the calibre of Caleb and Joshua. They may have been a tiny minority, but they followed the Lord whole-heartedly, and they got in when the whole of their generation lost out. Daunting problems were Caleb's speciality. He ate them for breakfast! When he saw a strongly defended mountain he didn't ask God for the route round. He said, 'I'll have *that*! Give *that* to me for my inheritance.' Moving on with God will mean tackling mountains.

'I can identify with so much of what you say. I have done all I know in my church situation and have lost faith for any change. But what am I to do? I know of nothing better around.' Is that your story? Commit your cause to God and he will surely show you his way. He may do a miracle in your own locality. Or he may tell you to get out, and move into the place that he has prepared for you.

'But that would mean giving up my job, and you know what it's like finding another these days. I would have to sell up, and we are so comfortably settled. It would also mean leaving relatives and friends, and—er—and heading for the big unknown.'

I'm sorry. I was thinking that you were a child of Abraham. Forget it.

12

WHERE THE
FIRST CHURCH FAILED

Jerusalem, theme of psalmist and prophet, is presented
to us in the Old Testament as God's earthly centre.
Similarly in the New, it was Jerusalem that was the focal
point of our Lord's earthly ministry. It was Jerusalem
where the grand drama of redemption was wrought out.
And it was Jerusalem where his followers were to commence their witness, and so reach out to the whole world.

However, reading through the Acts, we become aware
that a significant change has occurred. The centre has
changed from the Judean capital to a Syrian city never
before mentioned in the biblical record. We have moved
from Jerusalem to Antioch. At the same time the spotlight
has switched from Peter, the first of the Twelve, to whom
Jesus had entrusted 'the keys of the kingdom',[1] to Paul,
the converted Jew from Cilicia. The change is not explained. Are we to put it down to the inscrutable wisdom
of God who gives no account of his matters? Or could it be
connected with the mysterious title of this chapter?

The Criterion of Success

The opening chapters of the Acts constitute a 'success
story' unparalleled in the annals of church history. That

137

incredible baptism in wind and fire at Pentecost, the spontaneous sermon that produced 3,000 converts, the miracle of healing at the Gate Beautiful, the fearless testimony of the apostles before the Council, the mass healings in the streets, the opening of prison doors—as the irresistible tide of the Spirit swept on. What power! What opposition! What victories! We thrill as we read of the rapid multiplication of believers in Jerusalem, and even a great number of priests being obedient to the faith. 'Well, if this constitutes failure,' we may say, 'may the Lord give us a big dose!' But what is the final criterion of success or failure?

Acts 1 records how Jesus gave his apostles what has come to be termed 'the great commission'. The rest of the book is really the record of how they carried it out. First, then, we must look at the terms of the commission, and see how the first church fulfilled them, before we pronounce their record an unqualified success.

What were the terms? During his resurrection appearances Jesus spelt them out on four separate occasions,[2] so that the apostles could never have been in doubt as to what he had actually said.

According to Matthew: 'Go and make disciples of all nations.'

According to Mark: 'Go into all the world and preach the good news to all creation.'

According to Luke: 'Repentance and forgiveness of sins will be preached in his name to all nations, beginning at Jerusalem.'

According to Acts: 'You will be witnesses in Jerusalem, and in all Judea and Samaria, and to the end of the earth.'

Three facts emerge. First, their witness was to commence at Jerusalem. Second, it was to spread out in ever widening circles to the end of the earth. Finally, it was to touch 'all nations' and therefore to embrace all mankind.

The Great Turning Point

How did they fulfil the commission? As far as the first phase was concerned, marvellously. In no time the Jerusalem church numbered many thousands. Then there seemed a strange and unaccountable reluctance to shift into second and third gear, that is, to move out of Jerusalem into the regions of Judea and Samaria, as Jesus had commanded. Not even short sharp bursts of persecution could persuade them to leave. The church was now in danger of becoming inward-looking.

At this point the initiative seemed to pass from the apostles. They were still used, but not to spearhead the next phase. A new echelon of leaders, the Seven,[3] were appointed to serve the widows, but God had something much bigger in mind. Outstanding among these new leaders was Stephen, whose ministry was to become a pivot on which a whole new thrust was to turn. Was there ever blended in one man, other than the perfect Son of God, such purity of spirit, such heavenly grace and such aggressive fervour? Here we have a true radical of the kingdom whose meteoric course blazed across that eastern sky, not to disappear and be lost for ever, but to give light and warmth and inspiration to those who should follow.

After Christ Stephen is uniquely the 'full' man of the New Testament. Where other men were 'filled' Stephen was always 'full'.[4] He was 'full of the Spirit and wisdom', as were the other six appointed with him. But he was also 'full of faith and the Holy Spirit'. And then at the zenith of his ministry he was 'full of grace and power'. As had been the case with the apostles, great wonders and miraculous signs attended his witness.

His Finest Hour

Stephen's dynamic ministry stirred up the Jewish cauldron

just when it was settling nicely. Several religious groups rose up in opposition, but none could resist the spirit and wisdom with which he spoke. He was brought before the Sanhedrin to answer the false charges that had been brought against him. When Peter and John had been arraigned before that same high court, the man they had healed had stood there with them, but no one stood with Stephen. Alone, yet not alone!

What a scene in that courtroom! Stephen, his face shining like that of an angel, made his 'apology' without apology. His 'defence' was all attack. They hadn't realized that he was using the history of their nation as a sword, until at the end he thrust them through with it. They had taken their seats as self-respecting Pharisees and Sadducees, but when Stephen accused them of resisting the Holy Spirit and of murdering their Messiah they were like a room full of goaded bulls.

Inarticulate with rage, their jaws moved, their teeth chattered, but no words came forth. Stephen, wholly possessed by the Spirit, was seemingly oblivious to all around him. 'Look,' he called out, 'I see heaven open and the Son of Man standing at the right hand of God'[5]—as though the enthroned Christ had even risen from his place to acclaim and honour this faithful servant. But his hearers had now lost all control. Blocking their ears and bellowing at the top of their voices they rushed at him, dragged him outside the city and stoned him to death.

Why This Waste?

Why indeed, when a man was at the zenith of his ministry? Whether it is the costly ointment poured with prodigality on Christ's head, or a precious life like Stephen's seemingly 'thrown away' in his service, there is never any waste with God. It is just that heaven has a different method of computation:

Unless an ear of wheat falls to the ground and dies, it remains only a single seed. But if it dies, it produces many seeds. The man who loves his life will lose it, while the man who hates his life in this world will keep it for eternal life.[6]

As loving hands tenderly bore that body, bruised and battered beyond recognition, to its earthly resting place, who could have imagined how vast would be the final harvest? Radicals always beget radicals. Guarding the clothes of those who flung the stones was a young man in whose heart fell a seed. Try as he might he could not erase from his memory what he had seen and heard that day—a face lit up with heaven's glory; a prayer imploring heaven's forgiveness for those who were murdering him.

Every step of Saul's murderous path the barbs went deeper, until he was suddenly overwhelmed by 'the glory of that light', brighter than the noonday sun. There and then he flung his life down in reckless abandon at the feet of Christ, to become his chosen vessel and to bear his name to the uttermost parts. Then at the end, in some dark Roman dungeon, he too would pour out his life as a drink offering, as Stephen had done.

How many have been inspired to radical commitment by the life and death of Stephen. The witness to all nations that is to precede 'the end' will result in many more joining the Stephen company, those who overcome by the blood of the Lamb and by the word of their testimony, and who love not their lives even unto death.[7] And in that glorious triumph day Stephen will be there among the victors, the first and greatest of that 'noble army of martyrs'.

The Samaritan Breakthrough

The stoning of Stephen not only detonated 'a great perse-cution' against the church in Jerusalem, but a great spiritual movement to take the gospel further afield. 'All *except the apostles* were scattered throughout Judea and Samaria,' and they 'preached the word wherever they went',[8] undoubtedly inspired by the witness of Stephen. But why ever did the apostles stay put when everybody else went forth to witness to the regions around? Were they waiting for some word of direction? Jesus had already given it to them: 'When you are persecuted in one place, flee to another'.[9] This was not so much for the safety of their skins as for the spread of the good news. Later we find Paul obeying this very principle.

So the Twelve failed in this first instance to take the gospel to Judea and Samaria, as Jesus had commanded. In the event this was effected by the believers who were scattered, and in particular by the witness of one man. Philip was one of the seven, and therefore a close colleague of Stephen. What God had done in and through his brother, so suddenly and violently taken from him, had lit an unquenchable flame in his heart. Stephen may have gone but here is one man who would never be the same again.

Philip left Jerusalem and went down to Samaria,[10] and his obedience to God precipitated him into a new ministry. Philip the server of tables became Philip the evangelist. God was with him in power so that many Samaritans were converted, delivered from evil spirits and healed. 'Samaria has received the word of God' was the thrilling message that reached the capital, but the apostles had had nothing to do with the break-through.

Did this news remind them of their Master's command—'Jerusalem...Judea...Samaria'? Did it stir them to trim their sails and move with God? No, they were content to send a two-man delegation, Peter and John, who brought the Samaritan converts into the blessing of the Spirit, and preached in many Samaritan villages. And then to the regions beyond? No—they went back to Jerusalem.

First Missionary to Africa

The revival in Samaria was in full spate when God moved again without the apostles. An influential Jewish proselyte who was chancellor of the exchequer to the queen of Ethiopia, a man hungry for God, had been up to Jerusalem to worship, and was on his way home. This invaluable 'fish', waiting to be caught, had passed clean through the Jerusalem net. Would that have happened in those days after Pentecost, when the whole city was vividly aware of the presence of God?

Though Philip's hands were full with the work in Samaria, thirty miles to the north, God sent an angel to tell him to drop what he was doing and head south, past Jerusalem where the apostles were busy 'holding the fort', to Gaza, 100 miles to the south-west, and no reasons given.[11] With characteristic obedience Philip went. He led the Ethiopian eunuch to faith in Christ, baptized him, and sent him on his way rejoicing, to take the gospel to Africa. Heavenly transportation then conveyed Philip to his next assignment, and it wasn't Jerusalem!

'All Nations' Means the Gentiles

At last Peter is travelling around the country.[12] The miracle ministry of earlier days returns. A remarkable healing in Lydda and a raising from the dead in Joppa each results in a great harvest of conversions. Now that God has got Peter out of Jerusalem the stage is set for another significant break-through. The man with 'the keys of the kingdom', who had used one to unlock the door to the Jews at Pentecost, is now to use the other to unlock the door to the Gentiles.

We are familiar with Peter's vision and the wonderful Gentile outpouring that followed. Peter's opening words to Cornelius are revealing: 'You are well aware that it is against our law for a Jew to associate with a Gentile or visit him. But God has shown me that I should not call any man impure or unclean.'[13] This reveals what was the understanding of the Jerusalem apostles some eight years after Pentecost. They needed this special revelation to understand that the command to disciple 'all nations' must mean the Gentiles.

With the leaders still bound by Jewish prejudice it is not surprising that the wider church had no expectation of a Gentile ingathering. Those Jewish believers who came with Peter from Joppa 'were *astonished* that the gift of the Holy Spirit had been poured out *even on the Gentiles*'. It was one thing for God to visit those mongrel Samaritans —they did have at least some Jewish blood—but an outpouring '*even on the Gentiles*', that was staggering.

The news reached Jerusalem 'that the Gentiles also had received the word of God'.[14] The news did not seem to produce great rejoicing. The circumcision greeted it with mistrust and criticism. Peter was carpeted on his arrival and asked to give an account of himself. 'You went into the house of uncircumcised men and ate with them.' Fortunately for Peter he had a cast iron case. He could say, 'Don't blame me. It's all God's fault!'

What then had been happening to the church in Jerusalem? Certainly it had failed to move forward into Christ's great worldwide plan, but now we can pinpoint the root cause. Legalism of the Judaistic variety was 'the bird' that had never been shot and was now coming home to roost. There was now a circumcision party in the church strong enough to challenge the action of a leading apostle such as Peter. Because the apostles had not been clear in their own spirit over the question of Judaism they had not been able by clear teaching to shape the thinking of the church.

God Intervenes

While the apostles at Jerusalem had been dragging their

feet about moving out, God had acted swiftly and sover-
eignly, following the martyrdom of Stephen, to arrest
and convert the man destined to take up his torch. What
kind of a man had God chosen? He whose ways are not as
ours had selected a Pharisee who was more fanatically
Judaistic than any of the Twelve had ever been. As he said
himself later, 'I was advancing in Judaism beyond many
Jews of my own age, and was extremely zealous for the
traditions of my fathers.'[15]

But God had determined to do a radical work in this
man to root Judaism right out of his system. Hence he
records that after his conversion, *I did not consult any
man, nor did I go up to Jerusalem to see those who were
apostles before I was,* but I went immediately into
Arabia.'[16] There was evidently no one God could entrust
to share with this new convert the gospel of his grace
untrammelled by legalism, so God took personal responsibility for his discipling, and it was a full three years
before he set eyes on a Jerusalem apostle.[17] God was
forging a new instrument for a new beginning. For this he
also needed a new centre.

God's Irregulars

Only now do we discover that God had been at work to
break down Jewish prejudice in quite another quarter. He
hadn't waited for the man with 'the keys'. Way up in Syria
he had engineered an 'unofficial' break-through even
before the 'official' one in the house of Cornelius. It was
another direct result of the great spontaneous outreach
precipitated by the witness and martyrdom of Stephen.

Now those who had been scattered by the persecution in
connection with Stephen travelled as far as Phoenicia, Cyprus
and Antioch, telling the message only to Jews. Some of them,
however, men from Cyprus and Cyrene, went to Antioch and

began to speak to Greeks also, telling them the good news about the Lord Jesus. The Lord's hand was with them, and a great number of people believed and turned to the Lord.[18]

So it was Cyrenians and Cypriots, converts of those 'rank and file' believers that had scattered from Jerusalem, that took the gospel to Antioch. Perhaps they hadn't been taught the rules—'Remember, it's still only to the lost sheep of the house of Israel.' Or perhaps they just got carried away with the joy of the Lord. Anyway, for whatever the reason, they *'began to speak to Greeks also'*. So these young converts, because they didn't know any better, broke the Judaistic rules and achieved a breakthrough for God.

News of this great move eventually filtered through to Jerusalem, but not one of the Twelve came down to investigate or give direction. They sent Barnabas instead, and the heart of this 'good man', free of Jewish prejudice, was filled with joy by what he saw. Help was desperately needed. The obvious course was to go back to the apostles who had sent him. But he said to himself, 'No, I believe Saul is the man for this situation'—perhaps he was breaking the rules too—and so off he went to Tarsus to look for him. With Saul in Antioch God now had the new man in the new centre, and the stage was set for a new phase in the fulfilment of the great commission. Antioch even produced a new, non-Jewish name for the disciples of Christ, 'Christians'.

Antioch under Attack

Because of God's radical dealing with him, not only was Paul as clear as crystal on the non-importance of circumcision, but the church at Antioch was clear of legalism and enjoying full liberty. Satan did not like this and it was not long before this new freedom came under attack in the form of teachers who came from Judea insisting that people had to be circumcised to be saved.[19] Paul and Barnabas would have none of this, and there was 'sharp dispute and debate'. This led to the Council of Jerusalem where the apostles reached the decision that accorded with what Paul had been teaching and practising for years.

To Paul this was no peripheral matter but the very heart of the gospel.[20] Those preaching circumcision were preaching '*a different gospel*—which is *really no gospel at all*'. They were 'trying to *pervert the gospel* of Christ', and Paul viewed them as 'false brothers' and pronounced an anathema on them. He says, 'We did not give in to them for a moment, *so that the truth of the gospel might remain with you.*' Nothing less than this was at stake. One thing we learn from the whole affair. How far the mother church was behind the daughter church in Antioch. And the cause? The spreading cancer of legalism.

The Antioch Showdown

Soon after this Peter made what was probably his first and only visit to Antioch.[21] It was not an occasion of great joy, for Paul found it necessary to rebuke him publicly. 'I opposed him to his face,' he later explained, 'because he was in the wrong.' In the first instance Peter would have been taken aback on arrival in Antioch by the much more radical expression of church life there, with its total emancipation from Jewish tradition. The question in Peter's mind would not have been, 'I wonder what *God* thinks of all this?' but, 'I wonder what *brother James* would think about it?' James was now the acknowledged leader among the apostles at Jerusalem, and seems to have been an austere character. At first Peter took food with the Gentile believers, but when 'certain men came from James' to find out what was going on, Peter got cold feet, and refused to eat with the Gentiles any more. The other Jews followed suit and even Barnabas was led astray by what Paul described as 'their hypocrisy'.

What was behind Peter's inconsistent action? Paul's little phrase tells it all—*fearing the circumcision party*. Behind most legalism is undue concern about what others think. How dangerous it is and how subtle, that it could lead astray even temporarily such eminent apostles as Peter and Barnabas.

The Galatian epistle shows how antagonistic Paul was to every form of legalism. He uses the strongest language. The Galatians were 'foolish' and 'bewitched' to allow themselves to be influenced by the Judaizers.[22] They were turning back to 'weak and miserable principles...to be enslaved by them all over again'.[23] Anyone trying to be justified by law was 'alienated from Christ' and had 'fallen away from grace'.[24] In one outburst he calls the concision teachers 'those agitators', and says, 'I wish they would go the whole way and emasculate themselves!'[25] Hardly drawing-room language, we may feel, but something stronger than drawing-room language was needed to sort out the Galatian situation.

Curtains on the Jerusalem Church

Some years later Paul had come to the Jewish capital for what was to be his final visit.[26] James and the other leaders briefed him: 'You see, brother, how many thousands of Jews have believed, and *all of them are zealous for the law.*' This would hardly have thrilled Paul's heart. Here in the cradle of Christianity Judaism was as strongly entrenched as ever. Sadly these leaders went on to prevail upon this liberated apostle to go through purification rites in the temple for no higher reason than to prove to his Jewish detractors that the rumours about him were untrue. Paul submitted, and this resulted in his arrest, imprisonment, and ultimate transference to Rome. With this sad anticlimax to its glorious beginning at Pentecost Luke gives us our last view of the first Christian church.

So we see that the church's reluctance to cross the Jewish/Gentile divide and reach a dying world with the gospel was not due to complacency or lack of evangelistic concern. The church was generally fearless in its witness, with thousands of converts from Judaism. It was reluctance on the part of the leaders to allow the sword to cut them free, fully and for ever, from the legalism of their past. Though more than nineteen centuries have elapsed, and Judaism is no longer an issue, legalism in its various forms still is. For this reason that church of the first century has a timely warning for the churches of the twentieth century.

Seeds of Sectarianism

It is a shock to find that the seeds of sectarianism were there in the bosom of Christianity. The denominational spirit was incubating centuries before denominations appeared. Initially it was, as we have seen, a carry-over from Judaism, and it found expression in that pressure group within the church called 'the circumcision party'. Like yeast within a lump of dough it permeated the spiritual body, undermined the authority of the apostles, and impeded the growth and witness of the church.

Paul warned the Galatians that the Judaizers were not really seeking their well-being: 'Those people are zealous to win you over, but for no good. What they want is to alienate you from us, so that you may be zealous for them.'[27] They wanted to *win them over* in order to *take them over*. It was their own sectional interest that they were after. That is a characteristic of sectarianism. We need to enquire what lies behind what men are saying. Is it the preservation of 'the establishment'? Is it the continuation of human tradition? Is it the fostering of a party spirit? Those of us who belong to churches that profess to be New Testament ones are by no means immune from this tendency. The goal we profess to seek—'the glory of the Redeemer'—may be subtly replaced by another that looks identical, but which has self-interest at its root: the enlargement of *our* church or the prosperity of *our* cause.

Wherever a sectarian spirit prevails there will be little or no vision of 'the one body', so dear to the heart of Paul. There will be no passion 'for the scattered children of God, to bring them together and make them one'.[28] Instead there will be an attempt to defend or justify our denominational or other divisions. How beautiful but how rare is that pure devotion to Christ, untarnished by sectional interest, that characterized Paul. During his Roman imprisonment there were those with a partisan spirit, who were preaching the gospel 'out of envy and rivalry', intending to give the prisoner a rough ride. But Paul's reaction was superb—'Christ is preached...I rejoice.'[29]

The Elitist Spirit

Sectarianism invariably displays an elitist spirit, and Jerusalem was no exception. Theirs was not the elitism of a new spirituality or a new revelation—'we have the truth and you haven't,' but the vintage variety—'we have the traditions, the covenants, the law, the sacred writers, and remember, Christ himself was a Jew.' The Gentiles, newly converted out of heathenism, couldn't really be in the same league. This lay behind their reluctance to take the gospel to the Gentiles. This same elitism is evident today when people take secret pride in the ancient traditions of their church, and cannot in their hearts give true recognition to new churches that God is raising up.

Paul at one time took great pride in his religious pedigree: 'Circumcised on the eighth day, of the people of Israel, of the tribe of Benjamin, a Hebrew of Hebrews.'[30] What more could anyone ask? But the grace of God had thoroughly eradicated all that from his system. No longer would he put confidence in the flesh. All these things that had been formerly on the profit side of the account were now transferred to the loss side; indeed, he says, 'I consider everything a loss compared to the surpassing greatness of knowing Christ Jesus my Lord, for whose sake I have lost all things. I consider them rubbish, that I may gain Christ.'

Leadership Failure

When the shepherds give the lead the sheep will usually follow. God holds the shepherds primarily responsible for the state of the flock. Church failure is invariably leadership failure. We cannot blame 'the circumcision party' at Jerusalem. If those first apostles had been as radical as Paul in their doctrine and practice it is doubtful whether such a party would ever have existed in that first church. In the end it undermined the apostles' own authority and had a detrimental effect on the way the Jerusalem church developed.

The root of this problem was *resistance to change*. At first there were great changes effected by the spontaneous and powerful working of the Holy Spirit. But where would all this end? Was it now going too far? Would they lose all their Jewish heritage? Was it not God-given—or most of it? Would their fellow countrymen think that they had become Gentiles, and so become harder to win? In such situations we are all good at rationalizing. There has been a lot of rationalizing in the charismatic renewal to justify an unwillingness for radical change. It has been primarily a leadership failure.

How did the apostles justify in their own minds staying put when the church was scattered by persecution? Did they argue, 'We must not be pressured by this situation?' But who was really behind this pressure? Did they console themselves with the thought, 'It would be so much easier to get out. We are taking the hard course.'? Many ministers have told me that they envy the liberty that New Testament churches enjoy, but that they feel called to take the hard path. Yet whether it is easier to come out is questionable. One needs to ask those who have. But this is not the real issue. We should be asking, 'Which is *the right way?*' not 'which is the hard way?' 'To obey is better than sacrifice.'

Where is the Anointing?

There are leaders who feel quite sure that they are where God wants them to be. There are others whose hearts God has been disturbing for some time. It is to these latter I want to say that if we do not respond to God's pressures he has another way of speaking. We begin to discover that God is no longer with us as he was before. When the apostles failed to move with God he still used them in measure, but they were no longer in the vanguard of what God was doing. Their anointing had been transferred to others who *were* moving with him.

Stephen moved out and took the battle into the enemy camp, and God's anointing was powerfully on him. Philip obeyed Christ's command and took the gospel to the despised Samaritans. God was truly with him, and Samaria received the word of God. When at length Peter moved out the old-time power returned. There were healings and miracles and a great harvest.

There are leaders today who are saying, like Samson, 'I will go out as before,' but do not know that they have lost the anointing. One day they will meet someone on whom the anointing is resting. Or they will come to a situation where God is really working. They will then discover what they have lost. God will use this experience to make them thirsty again and to coax them out of their rut. The place of God's anointing is the place of God's appointing.

The Up and Coming

Young men like Stephen and Philip were unknown in those early days following Pentecost, but God had marked them out as leaders of tomorrow. He knew that the time would come when the older leaders would 'dig in', cease to move with him, and so become 'the cork in the bottle'. There are those reading this book who are the leaders of tomorrow. God requires you to honour and obey your leaders, even if you feel that they are the corks. But you do not need to let them cork you up. Stephen didn't. Nor did Philip.

We don't read of any leader telling Stephen to perform signs and wonders, or to dispute with those who opposed the gospel. But neither did anybody tell him not to. We don't read of any leader telling Philip to take the gospel to the Samaritans. But neither did anybody tell him not to. Both men were obeying God. Determine that you too will obey God, and leave the consequences with him. If leaders do stand in the way, keep your spirit right, commit your cause to God and wait for him to act. He may remove them—or he may remove you. Either way you will move with God.

To the Rest

You who do not feel that you are a budding Stephen or Philip, or indeed that you have any gifts of leadership: God wants you to know that you are of equal value and significance to him in the great work of his kingdom. 'Those parts of the body that seem to be weaker are indispensable, and the parts that we think are less honourable we treat with special honour.'[31]

Remember those thousands of believers whose names are only recorded in heaven, who were scattered in the time of persecution. They moved not in panic but in peace, not in fear but in faith, not in defeat but in victory. They were incorrigible witnesses who took the gospel not only to Judea and Samaria, but far beyond. Because they moved with God, God went with them. Make sure that you too are moving with God.

To evangelical believers, you who know that you are not in the blessing that you once knew when you were converted, God is signalling you to move—into the full possession of your inheritance in the Holy Spirit. You may be a Pentecostal or a charismatic, sensing that you have lost the freshness and effectiveness of your experience in the Holy Spirit, and wondering why. Is it that 'the cloud' of God's presence has moved and you haven't? You need to get back under 'the cloud'. Ask God to show you where it has gone.

The message of this chapter is that legalism is a major cause of dedicated and devoted Christians failing to move on with God, both individually and corporately. In the following chapter we will be looking more closely at this subtle infiltrater with his many guises, and finding out how to eject him.

13

GET RID OF
THAT SLAVE WOMAN

In the light of the history of that first church, as we have traced it in the Acts, it is significant that the seven letters written by the Jerusalem apostles contain virtually no teaching on the church. When we turn to the thirteen letters that Paul gave us we soon discover that it was the radical apostle from Antioch, the man whose emancipation from legalism was total, the great church-planter who took the gospel to the regions beyond—it was this man whose pen the Holy Spirit used to give us God's thoughts about his church.

Legalism is still Satan's most effective means of infiltrating and undermining the work and witness of the church. Paul meets this peril head on in Galatians, and so it is with this letter that we shall be staying for most of this chapter. If the reader could spare quarter-of-an-hour for a swift re-reading of it, that would be the best possible preparation for what we are about to consider.

The Galatians, having been converted out of heathenism, were now being sidetracked into Judaism. 'How is it,' Paul asks them, 'that you are *turning back* to those weak and miserable principles? Do you wish to be enslaved by them all over again?'[1] But how could they be *turning back* to what they had never been in? Simply this: 'the weak and miserable principles' are not peculiar to Judaism. Apart from the gospel, all religions of the world are 'law' religions.

These principles,[2] that have been defined as 'the rudimentary elements of religion', consist of rules that man is required to fulfil to find acceptance with God, and they depend on human effort for their fulfilment. This is why he calls them 'weak and miserable'. It is a slavery because they put man in the paralysing dilemma of '*I must*—and yet *I can't*'.

When they had first received the gospel, the Galatians had got off to a good start. They had begun in the Spirit. They were running a good race.[3] Then they had veered off course and got entangled with Judaism. They were behaving like a man with a life sentence who had just been pardoned, and who, when scarcely out of prison, behaves in such a way that the authorities are obliged to put him straight back behind bars. 'O foolish Galatians!'

There are many believers today in the same position. They too got off to a good start, knowing full well that they have been saved on the basis of grace. Like the Galatians they have also received the Holy Spirit by faith. But they too have been lured back into the legalistic slavery from which the gospel freed them. O foolish Christians!

A Serious Situation

In the days when new cars always had to be 'run in', a motorist, so the story goes, passed a new model travelling slowly, with the customary notice in the rear window, 'Running in—please pass.' Shortly after he overtook another car, this time going at a snail's pace, and the notice in the rear window read, 'Running out—please push!' The thing about legalism is that it cuts us off from the supply of the Spirit, and we have to maintain our momentum by pushing, and that's real slavery.

Legalism, Paul tells us, is disobedience to the truth.[4] God commands us to 'live by the Spirit',[5] and we try to do it by human effort. We are told, 'The righteous shall live by faith,' and we live instead by rules and regulations. Another serious consequence of legalism is that 'the Christ image' being formed in us by the Holy Spirit is distorted. 'I fear for you,' wrote Paul, 'that somehow I have wasted my efforts on you.... I am again in the pains of childbirth until Christ is formed in you.'[6] Perhaps most serious of all, and the Galatian letter makes the point very strongly, *legalism robs us of our inheritance*. That is the vital theme of this chapter.

Destined to Inherit

God never intended that our redemption should become the 'be all and end all' of our spiritual existence, as it seems to be for so many Christians. As the history of Israel's deliverance from Egypt shows, redemption is with a view to inheritance. He brings us out of Egypt in order to bring us into Canaan.[7] But the history also shows us that having been redeemed, the inheritance does not automatically follow. As an old saying puts it, 'There's many a slip 'twixt the cup and the lip.' A whole generation of Israelites, redeemed and in line for the promised inheritance, never tasted the good of it. They got out of Egypt, but because of disobedience and unbelief they never got into Canaan. They died in the desert. It was a new generation that came in under Joshua.

After the Israelites had spent thirty days mourning the death of Moses, God brought a wonderfully illuminating word to Joshua. Wait for it: *'Moses my servant is dead'!*[8] When God tells us something we think we know, it is time to think again. It *was* an illuminating word, for in it was the hidden key to open the door to the land of promise. God was telling Joshua that something more than a change of leadership had taken place. The old regime had passed away and a new day for God's people had dawned. 'The law was given through Moses; grace and truth came through Jesus Christ.'[9] Since the law can never inherit, Moses had to die. But grace, symbolized by Joshua ('Jesus' is the Greek form of his name), would lead the people in.

The Impotence of the Law

The law may teach us how to behave in the wilderness, but it cannot bring us into the land of our inheritance. We have only to examine the terms of the New Covenant to know why this is so. Three great words stand out, 'promise', 'grace' and 'faith'.[10] Let us for a moment contrast the two covenants:

The Old is a covenant of *commands*, the New of *promises*.

The Old is based on *merit*, the new on *grace*.

The Old operates by *works*, the new by *faith*.

So running like a thread through the argument of Galatians is the inescapable fact that the principle of law of the Old Covenant and the inheritance of the New are incompatible. This culminates in Paul's powerful analogy of Hagar and Sarah. It has all to do with Abraham's descendants, so we must first look at the covenant God made with Abraham, which Paul introduces in chapter three of the letter. This covenant involves us directly.

What Was the Promised Inheritance?

It was the promise God made to Abraham concerning *the seed* and *the land*, that is, Abraham's descendants and the land they were to possess.[11] The immediate reference was of course to the Jews and the land of Israel, but Paul gives this promise to Abraham a much broader application. God had promised that in Abraham and his seed 'all the nations of the earth' would be blessed. This, Paul explains, is being fulfilled in the conversion of the Gentiles.[12] All who are justified by faith, Jew or Gentile, are Abraham's seed, so that includes us. We are in the line of the inheritance, we share in the blessing of Abraham, who is the father of us all.[13] What an exciting prospect.

Then there was 'the land'. Just as Abraham's seed includes believing Gentiles of all nations, so *the land* is seen by the New Testament to embrace the globe. The promise that 'the meek will inherit the land' now becomes 'the meek will inherit the earth'.[14] The promise that Abraham (and his seed) would be heir to Canaan becomes a promise that 'he would be *heir of the world*'.[15]

We have thrilling confirmation of this in other prophetic scriptures. There were the Father's words to the Son at his ascension, 'Ask of me, and I will make *the nations* your inheritance, *the ends of the earth* your possession.'[16] This promise must be based on the covenant with Abraham, for the terms are the same. 'The seed' and 'the land' have now become 'the nations' and 'the ends of the earth'.

The Promise in Process of Fulfilment

Another promise given to Christ at the time of his ascension was: 'Sit at my right hand [the place of rulership] until I make your enemies a footstool for your feet.'[17] This statement, often quoted in the New Testament, is packed with spiritual dynamite. It means that the Father has given the Son a promise, and he is to remain at the Father's right hand until it is fulfilled. So it has to happen before he comes again, and he is now waiting for it in eager expectation.[18] We have seen that he was told to *ask* the Father for his inheritance.[16] As a king-priest he does this, ruling through his interceding. We join him in this when we pray, 'Thy kingdom come.' And so it shall continue, until heaven proclaims, 'The kingdom of the world has *become* [the completion of a process] the kingdom of our Lord and of his Christ.'[19]

The possession of the inheritance cannot be separated from the fulfilment of the great commission. We saw how the Jerusalem church failed here because of legalism. No wonder Paul is concerned when he sees this cancer spreading among the churches of Galatia. He wants them to understand that the law sabotages the inheriting process, that a legalistic people can never take the kingdom. Just compare the churches of the west, bound with their traditions and trappings, with the simplicity of the churches of the third world where the big advances are being made.

Where Abraham Went Wrong

This tendency to legalize was prefigured in the history of Abraham and Sarah.[20] It was just after that great occasion when God had walked with Abraham under the stars, and pointing to them had said, 'Count them, if you can, for that's how numerous your offspring will be.' Abraham believed God, and so God established with him an ever-lasting covenant.

It was at this point that Sarah began to reason it all out. On top of being barren, she was now well 'past the age of bearing children'. There was just no way, she figured, that this great promise to her husband could be fulfilled through her. Clearly God had a problem, and she would have to help him solve it. Her slave girl, Hagar, was the obvious answer. And Abraham, without consulting the One who was party to the covenant, went along with Sarah's idea. And so Ishmael was born.

This is where legalism broke into Abraham's relationship with God, and placed the inheritance in jeopardy. Here are the usual ingredients of legalism: human reasoning without faith; acting in the flesh instead of in the Spirit; trying to accomplish the will of God by natural instead of supernatural means. Remember, Abraham had begun well. He had believed God for the promise. God might now have asked him, as Paul did the Galatians, 'After beginning with the Spirit, are you now trying to attain your goal by self-effort?'

Where We Still Go Wrong

To many what has been written in this book regarding God's way for his church will be dismissed as idealistic, impractical, super-spiritual. They will tell us that institutionalized Christianity is too well established. A New Testament church today is a pipe dream. No leader of any stature would entertain it. In a word, it can never be. Then let us remember God's word to Sarah when, in her unbelief, she too laughed off God's promise to her as an impossibility: 'Is anything too hard for the Lord?'[21]

We are faced with a simple choice. Either we believe God for the supernatural working of his Spirit, or else we settle for legalistic substitutes, and that may mean simply perpetuating the status quo. Like Sarah's 'good idea', our substitutes will invariably produce something. Like Sarah's, they may even appear to achieve their purpose, but in the end we have produced an Ishmael instead of an Isaac.

Two Covenants and Two Cities

Let us now read Galatians 4:22–30, and observe how Paul interprets the story of Hagar and Sarah and their sons. 'The women represent two covenants,' the covenant of law and the covenant of grace. These covenants are 'mothers' who produce offspring after their own kind, the one a slave son and the other a free son.

They also represent two cities, the earthly Jerusalem and the heavenly. This gives the figure a corporate appli-

cation. It points to the church which John sees as already
in process of 'coming down out of heaven' from God.[22] In
contrast with this heavenly community is 'the present
Jerusalem' which is 'in slavery with her children'. Though
this has direct application to the earthly Jerusalem as the
'mother' of Judaism, it applies to all religious institutions
based on law. Whether a community is really operating on
the principle of law or of grace is determined by the nature
of its offspring.

A Community That Is Free

Freedom runs right through the argument of Paul's letter.
The free woman produces free sons. The slave woman
cannot do other than produce slave sons. Every child of
God has been born free. 'Therefore, brothers, we are not
children of the slave woman, but of the free woman.'[23]
But too many of us, like the Galatians, have failed to
'stand firm', and so have slid back into slavery. Others
again are imprisoned in communities that are legalistic.

Local churches should be colonies of heaven, miniatures
of 'the Jerusalem that is above', and providing on earth a
corporate expression of 'the glorious freedom of the
children of God'. This is more than 'liberty' in worship, in
the exercise of gifts or other congregational participation.
It is a company marked by a spirit of faith, a spirit of
grace, a joyous carefree spirit. A New Covenant community is marked by a spirit of lightness, without a spirit
of levity.

A Community That Is Fruitful

Having stated that 'the Jerusalem that is above is free',
Paul goes on to quote a prophetic word from Isaiah that
alludes to Sarah: For it is written, "Be glad, O barren
woman [Sarah]...because more are the children of the

desolate woman [Sarah] than of her who has a husband [Hagar].' '[24] So Sarah's freedom would be expressed by her *superior fruitfulness*. Hagar would be fruitful, but in Sarah's seed all the nations of the earth would be blessed. The one was a natural seed, the other a supernatural.

There is far more in this promise than an assurance that Christians would outnumber adherents of Judaism. That has long since happened. Isaiah was predicting that the 'Sarah' seed would outnumber the 'Hagar' seed composed of all in the world with a religion of law. The righteous would supersede the religious. This amazing prophecy goes on to predict: 'For you will spread out to the right and to the left; *your descendants will dispossess nations and settle in their desolate cities.*'

Abraham's Dilemma

Initially the birth of Isaac created no difficulties in Abraham's household. It was not until 'the child grew and was weaned'.[25] As he came out of babyhood and began to mature the sparks began to fly. 'The son born in the ordinary way persecuted the son born by the power of the Spirit.'[26] For some years a prophetic voice has been warning the church that a time of persecution is coming, just as the Scripture predicts. We should not be surprised if *graceless 'Christianity'* is involved in that persecution as much as Christless religion.

It was at this time of weaning that Sarah had something to say, and it was a strong word that her husband did not like: 'Get rid of the slave woman and her son.'[25] What is the problem, Sarah? 'The slave woman's son will never share in the inheritance with the free woman's son.' It was a radical uncompromising word, and one can visualize the jut of the old lady's jaw as she spoke it. We never knew that 'Mother Grace Covenant' could talk like that!

Now if Abraham had any weakness it was a soft-heartedness and a sentimental attachment to kith and kin. His obedience to the call of God both at Ur and at Haran was incomplete on account of this.[27] He failed to make a clean break, and his compromise only impeded the purpose of God. The issue was now surfacing again, and a fierce battle raged in Abraham's heart over Ishmael.

It was at this point God spoke. It was a word that no man likes to hear. 'Your wife has got it right. You had better do what she says!' He might have been excused for thinking, 'But it was when I took her advice last time I got into all this mess!' Now, however, Sarah's word had become God's word, and God had also explained what was really at stake. It was the terms of the covenant. 'It is *through Isaac* that your offspring will be reckoned.' All God's covenant purpose centred in Isaac, and in Isaac alone. This ruled out any compromise. There could be no sharing of the inheritance with that slave son.

It Begins with Recognition

One reason why 'Hagar' gains entry so easily to the lives of God's 'free sons' is because she is already comfortably installed, though unrecognized, in the churches to which they belong. How can we get rid of the slave woman when we have never recognized that she is around? Many are clinging to Hagar supposing her to be Sarah, and are highly indignant when informed of her true identity. As pointed out earlier, many things that go for church, a priestly order with vestments and titles, consecrated buildings and fixed forms of service, are simply Old Covenant forms in a New Covenant guise. Many will react to such a verdict, but only because they do not recognize 'Hagar'.

Take the influence of the church calendar on christendom. At Christmas time there must be Christmas sermons and carols. On Good Friday and Easter Sunday the preacher is expected to direct us to the cross and the resurrection, with appropriate hymns. Similarly on Pentecost Sunday. Preaching on these historic themes is needed, but why should the Holy Spirit be dictated to by a church calendar that he never inspired?

Why should we be required to commemorate our Saviour's birth on the occasion of a heathen festival, which has no relation anyway to the time of the year when he was actually born? Christians display 'the basic principles of the world', its legalism and its materialism, in the way they now celebrate this festival. Christmas is overdue for radical reassessment. The Galatians too had got caught up with a 'church calendar': 'You are observing special days and months and seasons and years!' says Paul; 'I fear for you, that somehow I have wasted my efforts on you.'

The First Day of the Week

The idea that the first day of the week is 'holier' than the other six, and that there is some special virtue in worshipping on that day, is another Old Covenant idea. A day of rest in seven, which many busy preachers fail to observe, originated with the creation and not with the giving of the law. It is still an important guide for our well-being. 'God blessed the seventh day and made it holy [i.e. set it apart] because on it he rested from all the work of creating that he had done.'[28] In this context 'holy' has nothing to do with the degree of sacredness. How could God's rest day be any more sacred than his work day? No, the word simply means that God reserved it for a special purpose. It was *set apart* for a day of rest.

We do not have any clear evidence that God authorized the early church to change the sabbath day to the first day of the week, in commemoration of our Lord's resurrection. On the contrary there is good evidence that God never intended any special day to replace the sabbath. The age for special days was over. After Pentecost the believers 'broke bread' in their homes daily. Was the act any more sacred or acceptable to God when they did it on Saturday or Sunday, than when they did it on Monday or Tuesday?

Sabbaths, whether of 'the-seventh-day' or 'the-first-day-of-the-week' variety, are a thing of the past. They are, according to Paul, 'a shadow of the things that were to come; the reality, however, is found in Christ.'[29] The sabbath itself was to find fulfilment in an 'every-day-of-the-week' *sabbath rest* of the people of God, and that means entering into our spiritual inheritance, both personal and corporate, as the letter to the Hebrews teaches.[30]

Elsewhere Paul both confirms and balances this teaching. In Romans[31] he equates the man who regards 'one day more sacred than another' with the man whose conscience only permits him to be a vegetarian. We should accept those whose 'faith is weak' and respect their scruples of conscience. Those who do not observe such rules should not despise those who do; and those who do observe them should not condemn those who do not, for God has accepted them. There is no desire here to attack those 'whose faith is weak', but to resist strong legalistically-minded believers who want to bring their brothers and sisters under a yoke that God does not require them to bear. Legalism is not so much in the practice as in the attitude.

The Subtlety of Externalism

We have already seen how the scribes and Pharisees laid great stress on religious externals to the neglect of inward reality. Almost all branches of the professing church are guilty here. Evangelicals, for example, have their own tests of orthodoxy and spirituality. 'Is he sound?' depends on whether he subscribes to a certain doctrinal stance on such subjects as the Holy Spirit or the return of Christ. 'Is she spiritual?' is determined by whether or not she uses make-up, touches alcohol, goes to the theatre and such like. Such tests are no better than those applied by the legalists of our Lord's day.

The taking of a strict line on these things is often 'justified' by the argument that we must not stumble our weaker brother. That is true, but all too often we act not out of tender concern for our weaker brother, but out of fear of our legalistic brother, and his strong disapproval. Such strong brothers need to be 'offended' in the same way that Christ offended the scribes and Pharisees. We do them a service by making no secret of the fact that we do not go along with their shibboleths and taboos.

Occupational Hazards of 'the Spirit-filled'

Pentecostals and charismatics have their own spiritual tests. When we make speaking in tongues the indispensable sign of the baptism in the Spirit we are adopting a position which can only be inferred from the silences of Scripture. Now if God wanted us to make speaking in tongues an infallible test, the 'silences' would be *utterances*, and what we insist is 'implicit' in the Acts record would be *explicit*. We fall into legalism when we take that one step beyond the word, or become dogmatic where Scripture is not. Even more so when we insert it in our constitution—another doctrine to which 'the faithful' must subscribe.

Parading one's piety before men is a kind of legalism that Jesus condemned in his day, and those who move in so called 'Spirit-filled circles' are as susceptible as anyone else. While serving with the British army in Egypt during the last war I attended meetings that some missionaries had arranged for the troops. In one of the prayer meetings a young soldier was 'groaning in the Spirit'. I had never come to close quarters with a Pentecostal before, but having read books like *Praying Hyde* I was suitably impressed. I needed to get close to this brother, I thought, and get my prayer life deepened. My admiration evaporated later that evening, however, when this young man came forward at the close of a simple message to 'give his heart to Christ'. I doubt that it was a first-time commitment, but I saw that the 'deep prayer life' was a bit of super-spirituality that he had picked up from older Christians.

At one of our Bible Weeks an earnest young man came to talk about his desire to serve God. Two or three times in our brief conversation when I said something that impressed him he closed his eyes, drew in his breath sharply, and shuddered. You might have thought he needed 'deliverance'. He did—from super-spirituality!

The habit of bellowing out prayers and prophecies (if you produce enough decibels to perforate your brother's ear drum you are definitely under a powerful anointing!), the oohs and aahs, the sucking and blowing and other variations that have been irreverently described as 'spiritual farmyard noises', the stock phrases and expressions that have become a mere patter, the view that if prophecy is to be truly authoritative or prayer is to be truly spiritual they must be in King James English, all this is externalism. The fact that it comes from the lips of those who have received the Holy Spirit does not make it acceptable to God.

We are not criticizing noise as such. According to Revelation heaven is a very noisy place. Half an hour's silence was so unusual that it got a mention in the record! But the noise there is inspired by the Holy Spirit. Noise of that sort will fill men with awe, and even draw them to God. But the other sort, performed by 'those who want to make a good showing in the flesh' has the opposite effect. It turns men off. And it doesn't take Spirit-filled men to tell the difference.

One could extend this list ad infinitum. We all need to pray, 'Teach me what I cannot see.' The important thing is that we deal thoroughly with every manifestation of 'the slave woman' that we do recognize.

Then Comes Renunciation

Having heard from God, Abraham was up early in the morning—always a sign that he meant business. He knew that the inheritance was at stake, and that put steel into his heart. *Cast out* or *get rid of* in relation to Hagar is strong terminology, both in the Hebrew and the Greek. It doesn't imply 'giving an invitation to leave', but 'giving a notice to quit'. Hagar and her son were left with no option. They were firmly shown the door. The radical Christian must face the same issue with the same resolution that Abraham displayed. His will must assent to a radical cutting off. For him too the inheritance is at stake.

The Death Blow

How is this radical cutting off effected? First we must understand what took place when we were converted. Listen to the testimony of that most legalistic legalist, Saul of Tarsus: *'Through the law I died to the law so that I might live for God. I have been crucified with Christ.'*[32] Death is the only instrument that can ever free us. And strangely, that death is brought about in the first instance by the law itself. It locks us up in conviction and condemnation, and then becomes 'a custodian' to lead us to Christ. Once we put faith in Christ we are no longer under the custodian.[33]

Now Christ has himself fulfilled the law, and also borne its penalty for us. Once united by faith to Christ, his death and resurrection become ours. We pass through death and resurrection into a new life. We are now born again— and born free! 'By dying to what once bound us, we have been released from the law.'[34]

'If that's what took place at my conversion,' someone

will say, 'I am not in the good of it.' Most of us are like the Galatians. We have been entangled in the legalistic net following our conversion. To come back into the good of it we must do what Abraham did. He received into his heart the word God spoke concerning both the slave woman and her progeny. There was an act of renunciation and of faith, and immediately a death took place deep within him. It was as though an invisible sword had, at one fell stroke, severed him from that mother and son for ever. This needs to happen with us, especially in relation to those 'terrible twins', pride and fear, the roots of legalism; and also in relation to the principle of self-effort which they engender.

Then one by one we shall need to put out of the door those personal 'Ishmaels' that God has pointed out. If we have got through with God and the work has been done in our hearts this is no great hurdle. We will know that the Son has made us free, and that we are free indeed. There will come a new release of faith, a new ability to possess our personal inheritance in Christ. Then we can commit to God those larger and more complex issues, the spirit of 'Hagar' manifesting itself in the community, which involve others. We may not know how God will work, but we will know that there is nothing too hard for him.

Let Laughter Return

It was not the cry of the newborn that brought the old patriarch hurrying to the maternity ward; it was laughter. Sarah was holding that tiny bundle of life in her arms when the full force of the situation struck her. Old Sarah in her nineties actually nursing a baby! It was ridiculous! It was hilarious! It was miraculous! It was God!

Through tears of joy and gratitude she looked down on that beautiful baby. All that God had said came flooding back. In those eyes she could see myriads upon myriads of glittering stars—mile upon mile of golden sand—nations waiting to be born—the seed destined to inherit the earth! She forgot all about the dignity that belongs to patriarchal wives. She laughed in sheer ecstasy. Laughed until her whole frame shook with it. Laughed until the midwives, servants and even Abraham himself were laughing with her. She couldn't help it. 'God has brought me laughter, and everyone who hears about this will laugh with me.'[35]

Two or three years later the laughter had died out of that home. There was tension, fear, insecurity. And Sarah knew better than anyone why it was so. We cannot blame her that she spoke so strongly. 'Hagar and Ishmael must go. It's the inheritance!' And God backed her all the way. Not until they went would the laughter return.

After Pentecost the Jerusalem church knew that compelling attractiveness of a joyous, carefree spirit, as they ate their food with glad and generous hearts, praising God and having favour with all the people. And every day the Lord was adding to the church.[36] But they lost it, and we know the reason why. The church of Jesus Christ today has lost it—if it has ever had it—and for the same reason. God is saying, 'Get rid of the slave woman! Give Isaac his rightful place. Let laughter return. The inheritance is at stake.'

14

THE LAND
OF THE RADICAL

God has redeemed us to be 'a people of inheritance'. Satan is determined to do all in his power to sabotage that plan, and as we have seen, legalism is the major weapon he uses to that end. But he has another weapon in his armoury which is a close second, and which requires us to be just as radical in our response.

When Paul speaks of 'God's abundant provision of grace'[1] and all the freedom that goes with it, as he does to the Romans, he is careful to explain what kind of freedom this is. It is freedom from sin, not freedom to sin. It is freedom from law, not freedom to be lawless. 'Shall we go on sinning,' he asks, 'so that grace may increase?' Or, 'Shall we sin because we are not under law but under grace?' To both questions he gives an emphatic—'*By no means!*'[2]

Galatians is the same. This great exponent of 'grace and liberty' devotes most of the closing section of this letter to a warning about the opposite danger, *self-indulgence:* 'You, my brothers, were called to be free. But *do not use your freedom to indulge the sinful nature.*' Then, having listed 'the acts of the sinful nature' (the lusts of the flesh), he closes with the solemn warning that *'those who live like this will not inherit the kingdom of God'*.[3] So it is not only legalism but self-indulgence also that robs us of our inheritance.

Modern society is motivated by a philosophy of self-gratification—'If it feels good, do it.' Being Christians does not give us immunity from this influence. But the Bible plainly warns us that to escape from the bondage of the law and be overtaken by 'the lusts of the flesh' is to exchange one kind of slavery for another.[4]

It is not so much the grosser forms of carnality that Satan uses to enslave us and rob us of our inheritance. More often the damage is done by those subtle and refined forms of self-seeking that our consciences allow. This is vividly illustrated by an event that took place shortly before Israel crossed the Jordan. As we shall be looking at this in detail it will help to pause now and read the account of it in Numbers 32.

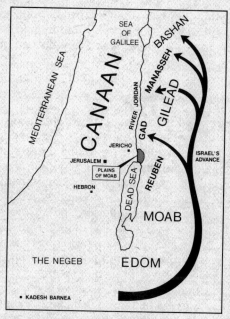

Israel's occupation of Transjordan.

On the Border of Canaan

In preparation for the conquest of Canaan God led Israel to subdue the lands east of the Jordan (see map), after which they returned to 'the plains of Moab' and camped beside the Jordan opposite Jericho.[5] This was the place where Moses gave his farewell discourses recorded in Deuteronomy. It was also to become the springboard for the invasion of Canaan. Only Jordan lay between them and the promised inheritance. There was a spiritual as well as a strategic reason why Israel had to come this way.

It was at this point that the two tribes, Reuben and Gad, later to be joined by half the tribe of Manasseh, requested permission to settle in the land of Gilead that they were now occupying. They put their case to Moses, explaining that they had large herds and flocks, and that Gilead was ideal for this purpose. 'Let this land be given to your servants as our possession,' they pleaded. 'Do not make us cross the Jordan.'[6]

The Jewel or the Case?

Moses responded angrily that they were behaving just like the spies had done by refusing to go to war and discouraging their fellow Israelites from taking possession of the promised land. The impact of this whole incident will be lost on us if we do not see clearly that the lands of Transjordan which Israel were now occupying, fertile though they were, were not 'the promised land'. It was Canaan, the land flowing with milk and honey, that God had promised. Again and again Moses described it as 'the land you are crossing the Jordan to possess'.[7] They could not gain this land without crossing the Jordan.

It was true that Gilead and Bashan were good for cattle. It was true that God had given them possession of these lands. But they were not Canaan. So these tribes were acting like a wife whose husband presents her with a valuable and beautiful jewel in a pretty little case, only to find that she has thrown away the jewel while highly prizing the case which the jeweller threw in for nothing! Had they gone for the promised land God could have thrown in Gilead and Bashan for good measure.

It is all too easy to be aghast at their folly while we unconsciously imitate it. 'These things happened to them as examples and were written down as warnings for us, on whom the fulfilment of the ages has come.'[8] Let us now look at the reasons for their decision.

Looking After Number One

Moses accused them of doing what their fathers had done at Kadesh Barnea. Surprisingly he does not refer to the disobedience and unbelief of that earlier generation, but of *their sin in not following the Lord whole-heartedly,* as Caleb and Joshua had done. It was in this respect that the tribes were like their fathers. They were not whole-hearted. They were not radical. Had they been so, the plea 'Do not make us cross the Jordan' would never have been found on their lips.

That Reuben and Gad should have been attracted to the fine cattle country in which they found themselves was perfectly natural, but it was at this point that they blundered. They failed to ask the right questions, such as:

What would be for the spiritual good of ourselves, our families and our descendants?

What would be in the best interests of the nation as a whole?

What has God already said concerning our future inheritance?

They never asked such questions because they were opportunists with an overriding desire for immediate material advantage. Self-interest, self-pleasing and self-gratification are all too common today, even among those called to lead the work of God. Such attitudes will bar us from possessing our inheritance just as effectively as legalism.[9]

Years ago I knew a wealthy farmer who was a Christian. He gave a fat cheque to a servant of God who promptly returned it, saying, 'Brother, you can't afford it; it's costing you your soul.' There are Christians ready to accept job promotion even though it takes them away from spiritual fellowship and church commitment and lands them and their families in a spiritual wilderness. 'But doesn't God want his children to prosper?' someone will ask. The answer is yes, but we need to understand what that means.

The Promise of Prosperity

In the language of heaven 'success' is to be equated with spiritual fruitfulness, not with material prosperity. If God adds material prosperity that is a bonus, but we will need to watch that it does not blight our souls. 'The Lord is my shepherd; I shall not want' is not to be interpreted as 'the Lord is my rich patron; I shall have all I want'. That wonderful promise, 'My God shall supply all your need,' is not to encourage us to expect a life of increasing affluence and an ever higher standard of living in a world where 'millions of people die of starvation each year', and where there are 'one billion people starving or malnourished'.[10] Such facts cannot be controverted, and provide every Christian with cause for sober reflection. How can Christians live in the lap of luxury and expect to have a voice to a starving world?

The Voice of Christ and the Apostles

Jesus himself set us no example in affluent living. His life-style was of the simplest. He warned his disciples against 'the deceitfulness of wealth', and how it could choke the word and make it unfruitful. He said, 'Blessed are you who are poor.... But woe to you who are rich.'[11] We have already seen how radical he was in handling the rich young ruler. It was after that young man had gone sadly on his way that Jesus astonished his disciples by saying that it was easier for a camel to go through the eye of a needle than for a rich man to enter the kingdom.

All this the apostles reinforced. Paul told Timothy that no lover of money was to be appointed an elder. He referred to 'men of corrupt mind...who think that godliness is a means of financial gain'.[12] Stressing the importance of a spirit of contentment he said:

> People who want to get rich fall into temptation and a trap and into many foolish and harmful desires that plunge men into ruin and destruction. For the love of money is a root of all kinds of evil. Some people, eager for money, have wandered from the faith and pierced themselves with many griefs.[13]

Poverty and Faith

If we seem to have piled scripture upon scripture it is only because many are propagating a message of material prosperity without ever mentioning what the Bible has to say about the perils. The New Testament encourages us to be 'rich in faith', and seems to link this with poverty rather than wealth. Paul refers to himself and his fellow workers as 'poor, yet making many rich'. Says James, 'Listen, my dear brothers: *Has not God chosen those who are poor in the eyes of the world to be rich in faith and to inherit the kingdom he promised those who love him?*'[14] This brings us right back again to the business of inheriting. Greed and avarice will disqualify, while holding earthly things loosely, and being rich towards God, will make us certain heirs of the eternal riches.

The twentieth-century church of the west seems to have a surfeit of those who are like the Laodicean church, rich in this world's goods yet poor in faith. If they would come out of spiritual flabbiness into robust faith they need to take a radical attitude to their 'excess baggage', and adopt a life-style more in keeping with the kingdom of God. It is said that when the Pope had shown Thomas Aquinas the treasures of the Vatican he remarked lightheartedly, 'You see, Thomas, we cannot say with St Peter, "Silver and gold have I none."' 'True,' replied the Dominican, 'but nor can you say, "Rise up and walk!"'

No Sticky Fingers

This is no plea to return to an attitude of asceticism that viewed 'living on the bread line' a virtue. But in the wealthy west the pendulum has swung too strongly in the opposite direction. Far too many Christians are without discipline in this area, and they need to know that they are putting their inheritance at risk.

It is not so much a question of how much we have, but our attitude to what we have. 'If riches increase, set not your heart on them.'[15] If some Christians have faith for ever increasing material prosperity that is fine, provided their objective is to *invest it in the kingdom of God,* and thus *lay up treasure in heaven.* This will mean that they increase the proportion of their giving, not their standard of living. Such a disciplined attitude will not hinder but greatly facilitate the spread of the gospel.

It was said of the well-known American evangelist, D. L. Moody, by one who knew him intimately, that although in the course of his ministry 'many thousands of dollars passed through his hands, none ever stuck to his fingers'. But how many other greatly used servants of God have lost their anointing over this very issue?

The Corinthians Got It Wrong

These believers were evidently prospering, but in a

manner that gave Paul no joy. Like some Christians today they had a totally wrong concept of prosperity, and Paul found it necessary to bring them up with a jolt. His words are potent, if tinged with irony, as he contrasts the apostolic life-style of himself and his fellow workers with that which they were adopting:

> Already you have all you want! Already you have become rich! You have become kings—and that without us! How I wish that you really had become kings so that we might become kings with you! For it seems to me that God has put us apostles on display at the end of the procession, like men condemned to die in the arena.[16]

Of course the Corinthians could not artificially create the harsh and hostile environment that these rugged church-planters had to face. That was not what Paul was suggesting. He was highlighting *a difference of attitude*. The one party had embraced the cross and armed itself with the mind of the suffering Christ, the other had not. To put it differently, the one had crossed the Jordan, the other had settled for Gilead.

The cross, then, is the only answer to these two major barriers to our inheriting, legalism and self-indulgence. By the cross we die to the law, and by the cross we die to the flesh. The plea of the Transjordan tribes was, 'Do not make us cross the Jordan.' The fact is, God never makes anybody cross the Jordan. You cross because you choose to.

Lack of Vision

One can only conclude that the Transjordan tribes succumbed to the temptation of Gilead because the vision of the inheritance had never 'grabbed' them. All the wonderful things that God had said about the land were no more than ideas stored in their heads which had never touched their hearts. Vision is what we see with the eye of faith. Lack of vision is a form of unbelief. 'Now faith is being *sure* of what we hope for and *certain* of what we do not see.'[17] Had these leaders been 'sure' and 'certain' of what God had told them about Canaan, could they ever have settled for Gilead?

As for the other tribes, their thinking was ruled by what God had promised, not by what they were currently enjoying. They were full of hope. 'The best is yet to come' was their watchword. Like Abraham before them, they were homesick for that 'better country'. Their God-appointed inheritance was no fantasy, no illusion. They had seen it from afar, seen it with the eye of faith, and that had spoiled them for anything else.

When one meets those who appear to have no expectation beyond an experience of renewing or refreshing as they pursue the denominational treadmill, one can only conclude that they have not yet caught a vision of their inheritance. It may be that God has given you some glimpses as you have been reading this book. For those who are giving this matter serious thought, here are a few practical considerations.

A Land of No Loners

For God's people today there is an immediate as well as an ultimate inheritance. The moment Israel set foot in Canaan they were standing on the land that God had promised them, and they could start to eat its fruit. That was their immediate inheritance. But it was only a small beginning, and there was a lot of fighting to be done before Canaan was finally conquered and possessed. That would have been their ultimate inheritance. For us, the taking of the kingdom (or the land) is a process, as we saw in the last chapter, and it will not conclude until heaven declares, 'The kingdom of the world has become the kingdom of our Lord and of his Christ.' That is the ultimate. But what is the immediate? How can we now begin to take possession?

Every Israelite who entered Canaan had to be *committed to a body* that had made up its mind to cross over the Jordan. Are you part of such a committed body? You cannot inherit individually. You may be hungry for God and eager for the inheritance, but you will never get far if the body of which you are part does not want to move. Let us be quite clear about this. It is the character of our corporate life that will in the long run determine the measure and momentum of our spiritual progress. It will not be valiant individuals but a committed body that will ultimately take the land.

Under God's Government

Loners are invariably people who have problems submitting to authority. Spiritual authority is not just a current 'in' thing in restoration circles, it is an indispensable element of the kingdom of God. Without authority there is no rule, and without rule there is no kingdom. It was an army under Joshua that took the land. Each man had to learn to submit to those who were over him. The coming of the kingdom today means the establishing of God's government throughout the earth, and that has to begin in the hearts of his people.

Joshua had his appointed officers, and through these delegated authorities he led and commanded his army. Similarly our Lord Jesus works today through delegated authority, through those whom he has gifted and appointed for different roles of leadership in the church. Only those whom God has chosen, called and anointed will ever lead a body of his people into their inheritance.

Many today have shrunk from involvement in the move of God because they were unwilling to submit to any authority except their own. Since we only have authority when we are under it, this has effectively robbed them of any effective ministry, and they have little lasting fruit to show for their activity.

The ascended Christ has now 'all authority in heaven and on earth'.[18] That means that there is no more to come to him that he does not now possess. That authority is the means by which Canaan is possessed, or the rule of God is established in the earth. How could Joshua have won the war if the people had not submitted to their officers, 'the commanders of thousands and commanders of hundreds'[19] that had been appointed.

There are church leaders, eager to move on, but they are under an ecclesiastical authority, whose major concern is to maintain the traditions, without any vision for the inheritance. And the leaders who want to move on, though they may seem to have complete freedom, will find when they come to make crucial decisions that they are fettered. Sooner or later they must come to terms with the alternatives, either to leave things as they are and settle for Gilead, or to take the radical step of cutting the shore lines and launching out with God.

The Two Forgotten Ministries

Among the commanders that our heavenly Joshua has appointed are apostles, prophets, evangelists, shepherds and teachers. The common theory that apostles and prophets are now defunct is as bereft of biblical support as the one that insisted that charismatic gifts have ceased. We will not spend time dealing with such arguments. One has only to examine what the Holy Spirit says about the purposes for which they were given to know that they are as relevant and as needed today as they have ever been.[20]

The real reason why apostles and prophets have not been recognized for so long is practical, not biblical. It is a question of authority. 'In the church God has appointed

first of all apostles, second prophets.'[21] These two functions take a place of precedence in the leadership of the
church because of the authority with which they have
been invested by God for the founding and structuring of
the church. It is impossible for them to function effectually
in denominational structures and do the job for which
they have been appointed without this involving a conflict
of authority.

Why We Need Apostles

There is a growing spirit of enquiry abroad concerning the
ministry of the apostle. This is not surprising, as he has
such a vital part to play in God's restoration programme.
As well as pioneering new churches he is able to lay
foundations in those that have none. He is gifted to re-
structure where the structure is unsound, and he has a
special part to play in bringing all God's people to the
unity of the faith, and so to mature manhood. This fulfilment of the prayer of Jesus in John 17 will never happen
without the effectual functioning of all the Ephesians 4
ministries, especially that of the apostle.

The apostle has a vital role in first recognizing, and then
bringing forth into maturity the prophets, evangelists and
shepherd-teachers. What the thumb is to the hand and all
the fingers, the apostle is to the body of Christ and all the
other ministries. The denial of apostles and prophets has
meant that the church has been trying to function like a
hand without a thumb and forefinger.

Where Are the Prophets?

This cry has come from the charismatic renewal with
growing insistence. George Otis, well-known charismatic
author and speaker in the USA, wrote in 1978 his reasons
for thinking the movement was dying. Among these

was—'An absence of the voice of the prophets in the land.' Since then Michael Harper in *Charismatic Crisis* has spoken of 'the dearth of its prophets' as 'one of the saddest failures of the charismatic renewal'.

From my own past involvement in renewal circles I would endorse this, but I have not found it true in those movements emphasizing the restoration of God's house. That with which I have been involved was born out of prophetic utterance, and has prospered by the same means. This was how God furthered the restoration of the temple under Ezra: 'the elders of the Jews built and prospered, through the prophesying of Haggai...and Zechariah.'[22]

'Men spoke from God as they were carried along by the Holy Spirit.'[23] According to Peter, that is how the prophetic word came forth. To speak from God men must be *where God is*. But God is never stationary, so the prophets were involved in a movement—'they were carried along.' The movement didn't exist to bring forth a prophetic word. The movement was on, and the prophetic word came forth. If no prophetic word is coming forth we should be asking, Is anyone around being 'carried along'? Has everyone dug in? Has 'the movement' come to a standstill? Has God moved on and left 'the renewal' behind?

When Joshua led the invading army across the Jordan the prophetic voice went over with him. From that point we do not read of a prophet arising in Gilead for 500 years, and as far as one can tell, not one of the inspired authors of the prophetic books came from east of the Jordan. Wherever God is moving freely the prophetic voice will always be heard bringing correction, wisdom, insight and direction.

It is my conviction that recognizing apostles and prophets, and letting them function, will yet prove the most important restoration break-through of our time. To inherit the land, we need to belong to a body that believes in them—not just in theory (as many do), but in practice.

Compromise Solution

The fighting men of the Transjordan tribes told Moses that, although they did not want a possession in Canaan, they were ready to fight alongside their brothers until each had received his inheritance, and only then would they return to east of the Jordan. To their credit these men fulfilled their pledge. They crossed the Jordan with the others. They saw and tasted the good land, but it never became their inheritance. Sadder still, their wives and families remained content with Gilead because they had never known anything better.

It is not the ground we cover or the territory we take, but the land we finally possess—the place that becomes 'home'—that counts in the end. God's command is, *'Dwell in the land* and enjoy safe pasture.'[24] This the Transjordan tribes failed to do, and sadly, that is also true of many whom the Spirit has renewed. There have been churches touched by the Spirit, some of them 'show-pieces' of the charismatic movement, but you would hardly know it now. While 'the move' was on, fighting men crossed the Jordan, but 'the body' did not go over, and so 'the body' never made it. In due course the move petered out, sometimes after the man God used went elsewhere, and the fighting men began drifting back to their starting place. This is inevitable with 'compromise solutions'. That's why they don't figure in the thinking of the radical.

Let off the Hook

You might think since Moses agreed to this compromise solution, it must have been quite satisfactory to God. Far from it. Here is the solemn lesson. Just as God cannot compel sinners to repent, nor can he force saints to be radical. He remonstrated with them through Moses, but when they backed off, God did the same. He let them off the hook. He insisted that they help the other tribes to conquer the land, and then, he told them, 'you may be *free from your obligation* to the Lord and to Israel.'[25]

If we know anything of the fear of God, those words should make us tremble. God released them to do the thing that was in their hearts, and never raised the issue again. There are believers today, and churches too, that God has let off the hook because they have not found it in their hearts to be radical. They may enjoy a measure of God's presence and blessing, but only God knows what might have been.

Victory—but No Beating Drums

Our Lord Jesus was 'crucified in weakness'. The cross is not only the antidote to legalism and self-indulgence, but the principle by which we conquer. The Israelites did not go through the Jordan individually but as a body. It is not crucified individuals, however numerous and however sincere, that will take the kingdom, but a crucified church. The victory will not come with beating drums, streaming banners or a show of strength 'when the saints come marching in'. The cross will always be weakness and foolishness to men, but 'the foolishness of God is wiser than men, and the weakness of God is stronger than men'. The cross puts paid to ostentation and display.

The book of Revelation gives us the open secret of the final triumph. Early on in the book we find John weeping uncontrollably because no one was found worthy to open the scroll of the One seated on the emerald-circled throne.[26] Then he is informed that 'the Lion of the tribe of Judah...has triumphed' and is therefore able to open the scroll and its seals. He turns to see this Lion and finds himself gazing at a Lamb. From then on it is always 'the Lamb' that he sees, in the midst of the throne, standing on Mount Zion, overcoming the armies of the Beast.

The word John uses for 'Lamb' throughout Revelation is unusual. It is the diminutive, strictly 'a little Lamb'. The Lion of the tribe of Judah, the One with kingly strength and authority, is 'a little Lamb standing, as though it had been slain'. The world gasps with astonishment. 'Is that really what your Leader is like? How pathetically weak and vulnerable!' Yet how true and accurate is the picture.

This little Lamb, with the stigmata of Calvary freshly and permanently upon it, slain yet standing, bleeding yet conquering, symbolizes perfectly the risen, ascended, glorified Christ, going forth to battle until all the kingdoms of the world are his, and all his enemies are made the footstool of his feet. And those with him—'called, chosen and faithful'—have also come the way of the cross, and are thus stamped with the Lamb-like spirit. The full plenitude of the Spirit's power is only released to the crucified church. In the famous words of Tertullian (c. 160-220): 'Dying we conquer. The moment we are crushed, that moment we go forth victorious.'

The Calebs and Joshuas

It is an hour of decision and destiny for the church. Growing numbers of God's people are coming to 'the plains of Moab'. Either they will move on with God, cross the Jordan and enter their rest and their inheritance; or they will settle for what they are currently enjoying, and cling to the 'safety' of that which is institutional and traditional, be it ancient or modern.

This is for some of us the moment of truth when we show ourselves to be radicals or compromisers. One thing is certain, God is going over into his rest. The question is, Are we going over into ours?

'Therefore, since the promise of entering his rest still stands, let us be careful that none of you be found to have fallen short of it.'[27]

NOTES

Chapter 1
1. Col 2:6.   2. Rom 12:2.   3. Rev 3:15–16 (author's rendering).
4. Rev 3:22.

Chapter 2
1. 1 Jn 1:5.   2. 1 Tim 6:15–16.   3. Heb 10:26–27, 30–31.
4. J. I. Packer, *Knowing God* (Hodder & Stoughton).   5. R. A. Torrey,
What the Bible Teaches (Marshall, Morgan & Scott).   6. Ps 4:4;
Eph 4:26.   7. Mt 7:3–5.   8. Deut 22:10; cf. Lev 19:19.
9. 2 Cor 6:14.   10. 2 Kings 3:7.   11. 2 Cor 6:17.
12. 1 Sam 2:12–17.   13. 1 Sam 2:29.   14. 1 Sam 2:27–29.
15. Lk 12:48.   16. Jas 3:1.   17. 1 Sam 3:1–18.   18. Deut 7:16.
19. Cf. Gen 15:16.   20. E.g. Jer 2:2, 20; 3:1–9.   21. Jas 4:4.
22. Mal 3:6.   23. Heb 12:29.

Chapter 3
1. The English 'public school' is a misnomer, confusing to non-British
readers, as it is really a private school! It is a fee-paying boarding school
catering mainly for the well-to-do classes.   2. Rom 11:22.
3. Heb 12:6.   4. Mt 23:33, 37.   5. Rev 6:15–16.   6. Mt 5:44.
7. Acts 7:60.   8. Jn 6:15.   9. Jn 12:20–24.   10. Mt 26:63–64.
11. Acts 23:1–5.   12. Rom 13:2, 7.   13. Jn 18:36.   14. Gal 6:1.
15. Lk 22:25–26.   16. Lk 19:41–45.

Chapter 4
1. 2 Cor 5:16 AV.   2. Deut 17:15.   3. Dan 2:31–35 RSV.
4. Lk 2:49 JB.   5. Jn 2:4 RSV.   6. Mk 3:31–35.   7. Lk 14:26.
8. Lk 9:62.   9. Lk 14:27.   10. Jn 12:23–25.   11. Lk 18:18–25.

12. Mt 9:2–8.   13. Jn 5:6.   14. Jn 4:46–53.   15. Mt 15:21–28.
16. Jn 6:66.   17. Mk 4:35–41; Mt 8:23–27.   18. Mt 17:14–18.
19. Mt 14:31.   20. Mk 16:14.   21. Rom 8:29.

Chapter 5
1. Mt 7:14 RSV.   2. Acts 5:13.   3. Mt 3:8.   4. Jn 4:16.   5. Jn 5:14.
6. Lk 18:22.   7. Jn 3:1–12.   8. Lk 19:8.   9. Quoted in Iain Murray,
The Puritan Hope (Banner of Truth), p.141.   10. Acts 1:4 RSV.
11. Lk 11:13.

Chapter 6
1. 1 Cor 10:2.   2. 1 Cor 7:14; 2 Tim 1:5.   3. Acts 13:24.
4. Mk 16:16.   5. Acts 2:38.   6. Mt 28:19.   7. Acts 22:16.

Chapter 7
1. Eph 4:5.   2. 1 Cor 10:1–2.   3. Acts 8:14–17; 9:17–18; 10:47–48;
19:5–6.   4. Acts 10:44 RSV.   5. Acts 11:15 RSV.   6. Greek *pneuma* is
translated 'wind' in Jn 3:8, 'The wind blows . . . .'   7. 1 Cor 12:13.
8. *eis metanoian*, Mt 3:11.   9. Acts 19:2.   10. Gal 3:2.
11. Acts 9:11–17.   12. Tit 3:6 RSV.

Chapter 8
1. Is 8:19–20.   2. 1 Cor 4:6 RSV.   3. Gen 3:1.   4. Dan 9:4; Neh 1:5.
5. Ezra 9:6.   6. Dan 10:11.   7. Ezra 9:3–4.   8. Is 66:2.
9. 2 Kings 22:8–20.   10. 1 Chron 13:3.   11. 1 Sam 23:2, 4; 2 Sam 2:1;
5:19; etc.   12. 1 Chron 13:1.   13. 1 Sam 6:7–12.   14. 1 Chron 15:13.
15. 1 Chron 15:15.   16. See Heb 8:5.   17. 1 Chron 28:12, 19.
18. 2 Kings 16:10–16.   19. 2 Kings 16:17–18.

Chapter 9
1. Ezek 13:10–11, 14.   2. Mt 9:16.   3. Lk 5:36.   4. Greek *sumphoneo*
(from which we get 'symphony').   5. 'The church' in *Encyclopaedia
Britannica* Micropaedia, vol. 2, p.921.   6. E. H. Broadbent, *The
Pilgrim Church* (Pickering & Inglis), p.148.   7. John Calvin, *Institutes
of the Christian Religion*, vol. 2, p.288.   8. David Watson, *I Believe in
the Church* (Hodder & Stoughton), p.333.   9. *Institutes*, vol. 2, p.293.
10. 1 Cor 3:9, 16.   11. 1 Cor 12:27.   12. 1 Cor 6:11.   13. Mt 13:38.
14. 2 Tim 2:19.   15. Jude 4.   16. 1 Jn 2:19.   17. See Acts 5:13.
18. Jas 2:2 (the Greek word translated 'meeting' or 'assembly' is literally
'synagogue').   19. Bishop Lightfoot on Philippians, quoted in *The
Protestant Dictionary*, p.534.   20. Heb 10:12.
21. See Howard A. Snyder, *The Community of the King* (InterVarsity
Press, USA) p.94; and David Watson, *I Believe in the Church*,
pp.248 ff.   22. 1 Cor 12:22–23.   23. 1 Cor 12:7.   24. *The Problem of
Wineskins* (Marshall, Morgan & Scott), p.157.   25. Eph 4:13–16 RSV.

26. Mt 25:40, 45.   27. Amos 7:7–8.

Chapter 10

1. Is 42:2 cited in Mt 12:19.   2. Mt 23:3.   3. Lk 13:17.   4. Jn 6:53.
5. Jn 2:19.   6. Mt 23:33.   7. Mt 11:28.   8. Lk 20:45–47.   9. Lk 12:1.
10. Mt 21:31.   11. 1 Cor 11:2; 2 Thess 2:15; 3:6.   12. *Encyclopaedia
Britannica* Mac., vol. 15, p. 994 (italics mine).   13. John R. W. Stott,
Christ the Controversialist (InterVarsity Press), p.70.   14. Ibid., p.72.
15. Mk 7:1–13.   16. Lk 11:37–44.   17. Mk 7:8.   18. Lk 11:52.
19. *Encyclopaedia Britannica* Mac., vol. 11, p.200.
20. T.C. Hammond, *In Understanding Be Men* (InterVarsity Press),
p.199 (italics mine).   21. J. B. Phillips, 'Translator's Preface', *The
Young Church in Action* (Collins), (italics mine).   22. Phil 3:3.

Chapter 11

1. David Watson and Arthur Wallis, 'Stay in or Come out', *Renewal*
magazine (Aug/Sep 1974).   2. Mt 21:43.   3. Mt 23:38–39.
4. Prof. D. A. Hubbard, 'Priests and Levites', *Illustrated Bible
Dictionary* (InterVarsity Press), Part 3, p.1272.   5. Bishop Handley
Moule, *Outlines of Christian Doctrine* (Hodder & Stoughton), p.214.
6. Eccles 1:4–8.   7. Eph 4:3, 13.   8. Jn 17:21–22.   9. Rev 19:7.
10. Mt 10:34.   11. Lk 12:49.   12. Lk 12:51.

Chapter 12

1. Mt 16:19.   2. Mt 28:19; Mk 16:15; Lk 24:47; Acts 1:8.
3. Acts 6:5.   4. Acts 6:3, 5, 8; 7:55.   5. Acts 7:56.   6. Jn 12:24–25.
7. Rev 12:11.   8. Acts 8:1, 4.   9. Mt 10:23.   10. Acts 8:5–25.
11. Acts 8:26–40.   12. Acts 9:32–43.   13. Acts 10:28.
14. Acts 11:1–18.   15. Gal 1:14.   16. Gal 1:16–17.   17. Gal 1:18–19.
18. Acts 11:19–21.   19. Acts 15:1–35.   20. Gal 1:6–9; 2:5.
21. Gal 2:11–14.   22. Gal 3:1.   23. Gal 4:9.   24. Gal 5:4.
25. Gal 5:12.   26. Acts 21:17–26.   27. Gal 4:17.   28. Jn 11:52.
29. Phil 1:15–18.   30. Phil 3:4–8.   31. 1 Cor 12:22–23.

Chapter 13

1. Gal 4:9.   2. Gal 4:3; Col 2:8, 20.   3. Gal 3:3; 5:7.   4. Gal 5:7.
5. Gal 5:16.   6. Gal 4:11, 19.   7. Deut 6:23.   8. Josh 1:2.
9. Jn 1:17.   10. Rom 4:13–16; Gal 3:18.   11. Gen 13:14–17; 15:5;
18:18; 22:15–18; etc.   12. Gal 3:7–8.   13. Gal 3:9.   14. Mt 5:5; cf.
Ps 37:11.   15. Rom 4:13; cf. Gen 15:18.   16. Ps 2:8.   17. Ps 110:1.
18. Heb 10:13; cf. 1 Cor 15:25.   19. Rev 11:15.   20. Gen 15–16.
21. Gen 18:14.   22. Rev 3:12; cf. 21:2, 10.   23. Gal 4:31.
24. Gal 4:27; Is 54:1–3.   25. Gen 21:8–10.   26. Gal 4:29.
27. Acts 7:2–4; Gen 12:1–5.   28. Gen 2:3.   29. Col 2:16–17.
30. Heb 4:1–13.   31. Rom 14:1–12.   32. Gal 2:19–20.

33. Gal 3:23–25 rsv.   34. Rom 7:6.   35. Gen 21:6.   36. Acts 2:46–47.

Chapter 14

1. Rom 5:17.   2. Rom 6:1–2, 15.   3. Gal 5:13–21.
4. 2 Pet 2:18–19.   5. Num 22:1.   6. Num 32:1–5.   7. Deut 31:13;
32:47.   8. 1 Cor 10:11.   9. Eph 5:5.   10. Ronald J. Sider, *Rich
Christians in an Age of Hunger* (Hodder & Stoughton), p. 13.
11. Lk 6:20, 24.   12. 1 Tim 6:5.   13. 1 Tim 6:9–10.   14. Jas 2:5.
15. Ps 62:10 rsv.   16. 1 Cor 4:8–9.   17. Heb 11:1.   18. Mt 28:18.
19. Num 31:48.   20. Eph 4:12–13.   21. 1 Cor 12:28.
22. Ezra 6:14 rsv.   23. 2 Pet 1:21.   24. Ps 37:3.   25. Num 32:22.
26. Rev 5:1–6.   27. Heb 4:1.